MIND *and* BELIEF V

MIND *and* BELIEF V

The Purpose of the Human Mind.

EUGENE BREEN

authorHOUSE®

AuthorHouse™ UK
1663 Liberty Drive
Bloomington, IN 47403 USA
www.authorhouse.co.uk
Phone: 0800.197.4150

Published by AuthorHouse   08/10/2015

ISBN: 978-1-5049-8871-1 (sc)
ISBN: 978-1-5049-8859-9 (e)

CONTENTS

SUMMARY

Everything in this world of ours is changing. Everything is aging and getting old and worn out - including the universe. This is self-evident. Everything we see or observe gets old and eventually decays. Nothing gets newer and defies the ravages of time. Our experience and the history of life over the centuries to date testify that everything is slowly but surely disintegrating. There is nothing in this universe that gets newer and younger and more beautiful as the years roll on. Or is there? No! There isn't. Plants and animals mature and die. The solar system is aging and scientists testify to its constant change and decay.

Everything tells us about this pattern of change. Our senses see change and decay everywhere in all aspects of life. We don't see permanent new things happening, we never did and never will. Our minds reason that man is a principal key to life because he is the most advanced being alive. We see that all men (and women) die and are forgotten and we conclude that "there must be more to it than meets the eye." There must be a reason for man and an explanation of what constant change and life is all about. Our deep experience of living tells us that we really crave happiness and that we only get a pale version of it when we love, when we give ourselves to others. Other human endeavours don't bring true happiness but a fleeting contentment. We intuit or desire a full experience of this happiness which is not achieved in this life, and we look for another existence for its fulfilment. Our knowledge of the gradual disintegration of the universe (earthquakes, tsunamis, storms, global warming, melting ice caps, solar change and increasing planetary distancing from the sun…) is a warning sign to us, that just as animals and plants decay and die, so too will the universe. This life is temporary everything tells us. Population explosions or heatwaves or ice ages are but deckchairs on the deck of this titanic dying universe. Watch out!

Did the universe have a beginning? It must have, since everything we know had a beginning and the universe is material like everything else. We don't know anything that did not have a beginning, or to put it another way, we don't know anything that is permanent. Absolutely everything in existence changes, and changes for the worst! Why do things do this? Why don't things just exist and stay as they were "originally"? Why don't they even get newer and more pristine? Given enough time the world as we know it will disintegrate, because that is the way it is heading and that is the way it has always behaved. Scientists confirm these constant changes in nature. The powers of change are universal, affect everything and are inexorable in their progress. We have never seen change in the opposite direction. We have never seen new material "appearing." The ginormous wheel of change is turning and the material world (which is fixed in its dimensions) is disintegrating. The scientists tell us the planets are progressively distancing themselves from the sun. The earth itself is part of this escape. It is becoming darker and warmer and losing natural resources like water and air and vegetation. Human activity is probably speeding up this process but maybe it is not the only cause. Maybe this is the trend of what is to come and is coming regardless of man's activity. Animal and human life come and go in flashes of time. The supply of animal and vegetable and mineral resources is getting less and less. There is no source of extra supply when they all become depleted. The world is finite and has not an endless supply of anything. We inhabit this disappearing habitat and *our* supply is also limited, like that of animals and insects. It seems that the limit of our supply (the future of the human race) is the capacity of the earth to continue sustaining human and animal life. There may be more to it, but it is obvious that there will be an end to human life also!

A disease could wipe us all out. A cataclysmic event could end the habitability of the planet. Man could become extinct, in the same way as he appeared in the first place – for no apparent reason! Man did not always exist. One reason for saying this is because the universe did not always exist. Cosmologists and scientists and even Einstein agree that the Big Bang is the most coherent and reasonable theory to explain the universe. George Lamaitre was the pioneer of this theory. A google search of his name will throw up more than enough information about the beginning of the universe and subsequent developments. It states that the universe began with a bang and has been expanding ever since. It didn't exist before the bang. Another reason for saying that man didn't always exist is because all anthropological evidence to date shows that man dates from such and such a date, and had a beginning in time. Another reason is because there is no other inhabitable place fit to support the life of man, and earth did not always exist.

The universe was not always there, as both science and scripture testify. It is surprising to some sceptics that science and scripture both agree about the Big Bang or the creation event or "beginning." The beginning of time has happened and we are all racing against the clock and we cannot stop it! Prior to the appearance of the universe and time you may ask "what was there?" The answer is we don't know, and to be honest we don't care, because we have enough in our own back yard (universe) to concern us not to mind going any farther afield. New things in this life resemble flashes or fireworks from a dying world. The universal clock is ticking and things come and go, as the poets say, in the twinkling of an eye. There is nothing permanent in this life. No science or art or human endeavour have ever found a permanent thing. They will not find one in future either because everything is under the wheel of change and time. These powers (time and change) do not stop or take a break. Everything in existence is under their starting orders. Everything changes all the time and time is a measure of this change. These facts are based on common sense and observation of the process of nature since it began, and on science. It is also based on the absence of any evidence to the contrary.

Let's discuss this a little more. Is a circle permanent? A material circle made of substance is not, since it is made of matter, and it is therefore part of the world as we know it. A virtual or imaginary circle in our minds is a concept or a form or an idea, and for existence it needs a mind, and a human mind is spiritual or immaterial and as such it is permanent, at least so it seems. Wow! We have already run aground with our simple statement, that there is nothing permanent in this world, and our entire hypothesis has taken a fatal hit! Not so. We will not get into the immortality of the spiritual or the human mind/soul just yet, but to allay any doubts that our original description of change is not correct, let us state that the human mind/soul did not always exist and therefore had a start date – with the birth or conception of each human person. It follows therefore that it can "not exist" and could "not exist" again if the powers that sustain it and made it, pulled the rug out from under it i.e. removed its life/being and so annihilated it. Philosophy cannot explain how a spiritual thing might cease to exist (because the principle of death is understood to be the dissolution of a thing into its parts and their corruption) - because there are no parts in a spiritual thing into which it can decay. Having said that it is also true that philosophy cannot explain how a spiritual thing comes into existence either! The human mind is not permanent in the sense that it always was, and always will be. It "wasn't" until we were born. Therefore a circle as a form or image in the mind is not permanent either. It is as permanent as the mind that contains it, and as we have seen the mind is not permanent. (At least it did not exist before we were born).

Taking the absolute opposite view to what we have just expressed about the impermanence of everything, and leaping into the ether of Faith we get an entirely different picture! This view says that *we* will live forever, because we were told so by God. Simple as that! We are also told that there will be a new earth, squeaky clean and never getting old or worn out. How about that! Either you *believe* that or you don't. You can marshal all the human science and ingenuity and knowledge, and you find that it all points on the one hand toward the decay and destruction of everything, and on the other hand to the dazzling magnificence of reality, and also to the faint silhouette of the master craftsman behind it all. The constant beavering away of man into the treasure trove we call the universe, and his uncovering or discovering of more and more amazing realities, be it the DNA sequence, or new galaxies, or the power of human love, begs the question "Who made all this, and who owns it? Where did it all come from?" Man has been at this searching and discovering for thousands of years and it will continue. The result of this quest is that man will have a perennial look of perplexity on his face unless he finds or "discovers" the key to explain it all. The *why* and *how* of it all.

We are not stupid (generally). We know when we are being duped. To tell man that "that's the way it is", or to say "we don't understand everything yet", or that "science will explain it all in time", is like telling kids that babies are dropped by storks under bushes! They are not serious and rational explanations. Getting back to ourselves and our destiny, the fact that we are partly spirit lends some philosophical currency to the reality of our eternal future, because we find it hard to understand how spirits die (according to human and worldly based philosophy). But alas, we were wrong before and we are constantly getting things awry, and we could be annihilated just as easily as we were created – spirit and all. The most powerful bedrock we have underpinning our understanding of reality, and the only one for that matter, is not science but religion. Yes, religion is the new "science" or vein of knowledge that supports and is the source of human knowledge. It is not new of course but many modern experts don't seem to have discovered it yet. It is our last chance saloon and the cast iron second opinion. It is the "phone a friend" who actually knows the answers and will tell you. We are all religious whether we like it or not! Fish and birds are religious in this sense too. They depend on a power to create and sustain them in existence. Man needs a power to make him and to sustain him. That is religion in clinical form. To get to the "empathic element" of religion we have to buy into it, get close and personal, and see where it takes us. In this sense religion is getting to know the power behind everything. It is getting to know and then to love that power.

This brings us to that other dimension in our lives which is the knowledge we learn or acquire based on Faith. Now Faith is not mentioned in psychology texts as such, it is not the subject of material science, but it is one of the most lived phenomena on the planet. With the gift of Faith come Hope and Love. These are the bedrock of our lives. Most people live these knowingly and many more live them unknowingly, that is they cannot put names on them but their lives are lives of Faith Hope and Love. Those that don't live these virtues or that reject them or deny them are missing out. These virtues are not humanly generated. Granted, there is a human and rational element, but their goal and ultimate essence is other worldly, supernatural and divine. It is the perennial science or knowledge that was always there and will always be there as long as man exists. It is a two way thing. There is man and there is God. Every other human intellectual pursuit has only got the man bit (of course God intervenes all the time to keep us in existence and inspire us and guide us but He leaves us free, and we could and many do "fly in the face of God"). You do need a helping hand in this business of life. These three virtues (Faith, Hope, Love) leave an after glow on the face of man and transform his otherwise two dimensional life into a three dimensional tour de force. They transform human life by injecting meaning and strength and the capacity to achieve what they intimate. Ask anyone who believes. Observe the lives and listen to the explanations of believers. They also make our lives into something lovable. They give a bird's eye view of who we are, why we are in the state we are in, and what purpose of our lives have. They point to the tremendous future in store for those who follow their path. They paint the story of man as it really is. They elevate it beyond our wildest happiest dreams. In human life people often "go it alone" and survive. Most serious tasks like climbing Everest demand a team effort and a lot of know-how. "Life" isn't a go it alone project. Without the code or the key you cannot see the whole picture and you cannot gain access to the grand stand. Without God's "OK", we are at nothing. We are doomed to spend our lives wandering aimlessly through the maize and never finding the opening to real life. We are unintelligible beings without God. We mean nothing. You have to ask how we exist at all without a creator and sustainer.

Every person is just that – a person. Some are intelligent and some are philosophers and some are mystics, but all are at the same level of being. We are all in this together and we grope around sifting through science and thought and experience, to try and come up with some answers to the meaning of life. We could all be wrong! A bunch of computer illiterates let loose on a 5 or 6 series smart phone might conclude it is a fancy door stop, unless someone gets inspired and switches it on and swipes the screen - otherwise it is still a dead bit of plastic. A computer kid can show what the smart phone can do in minutes. We are such "life" illiterates and unless someone gets inspired and switches us on and swipes us we are dead matter. We need a computer expert, and even better if we get the creator of our computer, who can explain to us how we work. Without this external incontrovertible second opinion from a certified expert we are lost. A power above human intelligence is needed to give this second opinion. Millions of people say God is this expert and He has told us the story.

Yes we have been told the story and we understand the message in our deepest selves….but do we believe what we are told by the all-powerful creator? Is it trustworthy and credible and in keeping with our rationality? Yes, yes and yes. If not we are in denial. Everything has a cause. Our reason tells us this. Our very lives tell us this. God tells us this. Our rationality is reliable and vouched for when used honestly and followed through to where it leads. Life shows this. If this were not so we would have no basis for philosophy or science or anything. Being honest and open to what correct reason says when unhindered by agendas and biases is our true modus operandi. Our reason tells us that everything has a cause. Just think if there is anything that really happens spontaneously without a cause. The answer is no there is not. Our minds are hard wired to causality and everything we do when based on causality and rationality in this life works – provided the reason is correct.

Time is a measure of the change in everything. Time does not exist per se as an independent real entity but is a human experience or measure of change. Everything changes. There is no permanent or unchanging substance or reality in this world. There isn't because it would contradict the blueprint of life revealed by science and scripture. (Life has a beginning and end, and the world is temporary. Something permanent in this life, would contradict the temporariness of everything and make null the philosophy of reason and the meaning of everything!).

This small book is not a novella. It is more like a depth charge! It pokes around at the roots of life and man and woman, and mixes the sublime with the ridiculous. It is like a witch (or even better), an alchemist stirring a brew on sizzling coals, which low and behold produces a magnificent vapour from the pot, which turns into a beautiful image of life and of man and woman dancing away into the perennial sunset! That is the plan. It is not an easy read. It is meant to provoke ideas and impressions and reactions, which in their turn may spur one on to a new and better way of seeing life and living life and forging onward toward a better future. This is the goal let's see if you agree!

Many other aspects of man's experiences - from death to love to suffering to delusion have been covered in the previous book "Mindandbelief.com". The present offering is an extension of the previous books under the same title –

The Human Mind and Belief 1 – Opening Shots;
The Human Mind and Belief II – Unplugged;
The Human Mind and Belief III – Reloaded;
Mindandbelief.com. IV

Join the discussion at email: mindandbelief@gmail.com

INTRODUCTION

The world of the mind and the heart of man and woman is a sea without shores. It is a world of joy and tragedy. It has untold hopes and possibilities, and depths of suffering and depravity. Who is qualified to write about it? Who can step up to the plate? Could you say that everyone with a mind and heart is qualified to write about it, and to express their emotions and thoughts? The answer is yes. Most people understand these ideas. People who are incapacitated in some way and are unable to express or connect with their thoughts may not be able. Not everyone has the capacity to put into words what they feel or think. Anyone who has lived a life does have something to say. They are qualified to get a hearing, and with respect, because of their dignity as persons and their effort and time spent living their lives. Everyone is a philosopher. Everyone is a psychologist. Everyone experiences another life "far from the madding crowd" (Thomas Hardy's novel) deep in the privacy of their own hearts. These are their credentials for speaking about life and heart and mind. Artists do it with paints and pictures. Composers do it with music and song. Writers do it with fiction and fantasy and poetry and non-fiction. This book is non-fiction.

The analysis of human thought and behaviour usually requires a person to have had a broad experience of life, (usually, though Emily Bronte for example wrote Wuthering Heights when she was only 29 and there are many other young wise people), and a good grasp of what it means to be human. Everyone has their own world view or prism through which they view life. It is true to say that this view can and does colour their understanding of human nature and the meaning of life. If for example you asked an atheist, a Buddhist and a Catholic to write a book about life, they would have very different views about many things. You could pick well educated people with access to modern science and internet information - yet their assessments of life would be very varied and even contradictory. All you have to do is read books by such people and you will easily see the disparities and contradictions. Atheists believe (is that the right word?) that what you see is what you get. There is no God. There is no creation. There is no hope. There is no afterlife. Live life, for tomorrow you will die. Buddhists believe in an atheistic religion or view of life where process is the way and reincarnation is for everyone. They base their lives on the writings of Buddha who is reputed to have lived 4 to 6 centuries BC. The goal is to achieve Nirvana or inner peace. Catholics accept science literature and art and all honest things as coming from the hands of God. They believe in a personal God who lived among us for 33 years. Creation and eternity and justice and punishment are key truths of this faith.

Imagine these three experts in a pub discussing Barclay's Premier League! No problem! Imagine them discussing the Mona Lisa, probably no problem either. Imagine them discussing the meaning of man/woman. Big issues! Their basic concepts of the human person are almost polar opposites. Yet they can't all be right. A football is a football no matter what anyone thinks about it. A window is a window regardless of human thought or belief. A set of dentures is a set of dentures even if someone writes a book about them. I, with my mind, and you with yours cannot touch or affect a change in these things (so it seems and we will return to this idea a little later). Does it really matter what anyone thinks or believes? Of course it matters to the individual, because the belief system impacts profoundly on their lives and their happiness and their way of living. But does what we think affect anything outside ourselves - in themselves? The point being pursued here is whether it matters to reality or to life and its origins and underpinnings that we think or believe anything. Does it matter to God if an atheist does not believe in God? Does that change anything? Won't God continue to be God regardless of how many atheists there are? If I believe footballs don't exist and millions believe the same will that affect footballs? No, if footballs exist (and they do) what anyone thinks doesn't affect their reality and existence. Similarly world views differ remarkably and yet the world is as it is and our thought will not change anything (Yea?). A thing or reality is what it is regardless of human opinion. Therefore to continue this line of discussion, if the universe is created and has a best-by date ready to destruct in time and is all guided by the hand of God, well, end of discussion, that's it. It really doesn't matter what anyone thinks. What *is*, is, and it is our problem if we have gotten it wrong and think or believe everything is the opposite of what it really is. Alternatively, if the universe and man are automatically evolving phenomena with no beginning and no end (and no meaning!) well then try explaining what it is all supposed to mean. A third way could be the never ending wheel of life with some realities of a spiritual nature intermixed with animal man and the universe in a totality of being, achieving some peace of mind. Whatever that is!

Now which one is it, or is it a mixture of a few processes? This is not meant to be a discourse about the proofs of the existence of God. It is being discussed so that people can think about what *could* be, and what *is* true. There can be and often is a partial truth. There can be real bits and false bits. There can also be the genuine article and the total real truth. Atheist, Buddhist, and Catholic cannot all be right about everything because they contradict each other. The best answer to issues such as opposing opinions in a table quiz for example is for the quiz master to reveal the answer. Ultimately there can only be one truth, because if there are more than one they will agree and so again there will only be one, and if they disagree they cannot both be true and so one is wrong. It is also true that there are many paths to the truth. What will not work would be a path going in the opposite direction. All paths that eventually lead to truth are complimentary or compatible. They are not opposed. Atheism and theism are going in opposite directions and both cannot be right.

The fact that you or I think and even believe that a house is bugged doesn't affect the house. If it is bugged it is bugged and if not well then it isn't. But maybe it isn't that simple! If we think the house is bugged we might leave the house, we might clean it out and investigate to find the bug, or we might put up screens to prevent speech or vision accessing the bugs. All these changes would affect the house. So what we believe does have down stream effects on the house. Our belief system is powerful and it effects change. This seems to only apply when we can actually make a change to a thing or a situation within our influence. No matter what we may think or believe about the moon or any planet it will not affect the planet. It will continue to be as it is. No matter what we believe about Scunthorpe United football team it will not affect the team, unless we buy it or publish articles about it or whatever. But realistically speaking we cannot affect the football team. Things within our ambit and locus of control or influence may be affected by our beliefs. As such belief is not an inert activity confined to the mind of an individual. This seems to contradict what we said above about windows and footballs not being affected by a person's belief. Let us continue to tease it out. If you believe a person within your circle is a very decent character this will affect your dealings with that person, and also what you say about him. Also, if you believe a person is a swindler and thief this will have the opposite effect on your relationship with him. If you believe the supermarket owner loves you this definitely will affect you. You might try to meet him and respond to his love. You might spend a lot of time dwelling on the "fact" that he loves you. You might even ask him out. These situations arise all the time!

Our beliefs definitely affect us - ourselves. Our beliefs can have knock on effects on others or even on things when we act on our beliefs about them. Could you say that our beliefs actually bring about change outside our own heads? Yes! If belief was a circumscribed experience in a person's head it would be a dead thing in a certain sense. It would not impact on life outside the person. Beliefs really do impact on life. A person who believes the sun shines in Spain will want to holiday there. A person who believes someone double crossed him will want to get revenge. A person who believes in a religion will manifest the tenets of that faith in society. Look at all the wars and killings and charity works done in the name of belief. This is an enormous reality in life, based on *belief.* The present wars in Syria and neighbouring places are based on beliefs. The present ideology and world views expressed by the world press are couched in belief of atheistic world views. The entire media and means of communications are seriously biased toward a materialistic agnostic belief system. Beliefs do affect people and others and life. Your belief about anything can affect your interaction with that thing and that can change it.

Is everything then subject to our belief? No has to be the answer. What the reach of our belief is, is anybody's guess. What we cannot do is change the truth, or the reality of things by our belief. "Why not and how do you know?" You may ask. This begs the question "What is truth?" It also begs the question "What is belief and is all belief the same and just different versions of the same phenomenon?" The school boy's answer to truth is "truth is the way things are" and it doesn't get better or more profound than that. We don't really know what truth is because we didn't invent or create it. We are given fundamental instincts and insights and reason, and if we doubt these we are stupid and mistaken. Without accepting some basis, you cannot move on or rationalise or think. Without accepting a nugget of truth to work with as a basis we cannot know and will never know anything. The history of man shows that the entire edifice of human endeavour, be it science or literature or art is built completely on the foundation of given first principles. These are: the veracity of our rationality (that what our minds and our reason deduce and think can be true and is true when these faculties are used honestly and simply and without deception); the reality of causality (everything is caused by something else); the truthfulness of our senses (what they convey are real and true images or imprints of reality); the existence of free will and personal responsibility of the individual. These are the building blocks without which we cannot think or build or progress.

The history and advancement of humanity to date are based on free will, cause and effect, rationality and the acceptance of the truth of the world and of our senses and our minds. These are sine qua non fundamental first principles that humanity to date has accepted and successfully built on. How do you advance beyond the animals without these principles? Why have animals not moved on from the tree and the den and the coral reef? Maybe its because they don't think rationally! Man has thought rationally since time began because its his nature to think rationally and also because it works. The present world of internet and science and medicine all need cause and effect as a basic tool to understand what they are doing and to advance science. A doctor uses cause and effect to see why a patient is suffering. The legal system uses cause and effect to see who is guilty or innocent. Nothing on this earth or anywhere happens without a cause. No one has ever seen anything happen without a cause. It is impossible.

Truth is the way things really are. Truth `for us` is our grasp of this reality without changing its true content. We can lie and dissimulate and we are biased and subject to error and deceit and passions, and we can and often do twist the truth. We like to see things the way we want to see them. It suits us. We find truth difficult because we find it difficult to live up to the truth. When truth is neutral like a football or a shovel or sunshine, that's ok. When truth challenges us and forces us to change our lives, then we can deceive ourselves and not accept it or deny or alter the truth. Such a truth is at risk in us. We all experience this. "You drink too much. No I don't." (When in fact you drink way too much). "That cough is due to cigarettes. No it isn't." (When it is causing bronchitis). There are over 50 types of bias and these are just the start of how we can spin the truth to suit our needs. A simple rationality like that of a child who says it as it is, and when it finds the truth too hard to bear, asks for help, is the honest and best way to live. It ensures that we live in the truth and not in bits of the truth or in what our mind tells us is true. We cannot change the truth but we can alter it in our own heads. Then the truth is still the truth but our imprint of what is true is wrong. This erroneous concept of truth then affects our behaviour and our thoughts. We become deluded. The worst of all scenarios is when we become chronically deluded about ourselves and about life. The virtue of humility which is the ability to accept and understand ourselves as we really are, warts and all, is a great antidote to this type of delusion.

To recap, the reason we cannot change the truth with our belief is because genuine *belief is at the service of truth*. The human faculty of belief only kicks in when the object of that belief is taken to be true. You cannot *believe* in something you know is untrue. Just try! You believe what your wife or friend tell you because you think they are honest and would not deceive you, and therefore what they tell you is true. The ultimate belief is belief in God and it is similar. You believe what He tells you because "He cannot deceive or be deceived" - so says the penny catechism. Also truth originates beyond us. We cannot touch it. The only one who can touch truth is the maker of truth. The only one who can change the laws of nature for example is the maker of the laws. No matter how much you dislike gravity or the spin of the earth or the movement of the oceans there is nothing you can do about them. They are fixed and we didn't fix them. Whoever fixed them may have the power to change them. Similarly the truth of reality is fixed and we have to respect that and work with it. Changing things as we do every day and as the entire universe does every second is not changing the truth. It is respecting the reality and truth of things and changing their presentation into other different realities or truths. Nothing is created or annihilated and there is no magic. A cigarette is changed into ash by combustion. A face is changed by a smile. A smiling face is as real as a serious face, and what happens is that one true thing is changed into another true thing. In this case it is humour not combustion that brings about change. Both are real and true. In this world being true and real doesn't mean reality cannot change. As mentioned above the entire world is in a constant state of change from planetary movement to weather to the oceans to man. Everything changes and everything is true and real. These are fundamental principles accepted and built on by all reliable philosophers and scientists and intellectuals and children to date. The key thing for us is that we say things as they *are* and acknowledge the real truth of things and situations.

The previous discussion was apropos of the statement that "our belief cannot change the truth." We said the truth is the "way things are". We did not make things or create things. We inherited the planet and everything was "all up and running" when we arrived. We fell on our feet and just took over and discovered what was already in existence. "We inherited the earth." What belief does do is to get us to effect change to things and persons through our own persons as instruments and influence. Examples mentioned above include our attitude to persons, or our ideas about a house or our beliefs about the supermarket owner. Belief therefore harnesses us to get active.

People often publicise their world views and beliefs, or their lack of belief, and as a result influence many people – proving that belief also acts outside the believing person. Consider all the atheistic "best sellers" and the power of marketing to promote an agenda like: "There is no God" (Dawkins, Hawking, others). The lives of true believers and the impact they had on people and the world is amazing. Martin Luther King, St John Paul II, Aleksandr Solzhenitsyn, Mother Teresa to mention a few have improved the lives of millions of people. Belief is a truly great power that reaches the ends of the earth in some special people as proven by their real influence on countless others for the better. This belief originates in the mind/soul of an individual. A contemplative who spends all day every day praying or contemplating is activated very powerfully by belief - they are so activated that they spend their entire lives closeted away talking to God. Who else would do this and for what reason? It must be a powerful strength and motivation to achieve a lifelong endurance like that. It also asks the question "how does their life of belief affect the world and others?" Believers know it does through their belief and the knowledge this gives, but unbelievers want evidence. The big ticket believers mentioned above (St John Paul, Mother Teresa…) have documented evidence of colossal effects caused by their lives of belief, and the smaller fish who believe may not be able to grandstand such results, but it is the same power and it surely has effects proportionate to the believer's Faith. It is not the brief of this book to demonstrate the effectiveness of belief. Suffice it to say there is abundant evidence and each person can research this themselves.

To be an atheist you really need a pile of faith - to actually grasp and accept and *believe* that the life which we experience and live in the animal dimension is all that there is. To believe that the whirlwind of human joy and tragedy is either meaningless or is completely resolved in this life …is amazing! What remains in an atheistic world is a frantic need to fill the vacuum of meaning in life.

Let us then pose the key question "can you have truth?" Can you cut out the agendas and overt or subliminal biases, and display the actual truth of life without bias or interference? The answer is yes. What you can do is progress with the simplicity of a child and call things by their names, and build one block on another and bring everyone with you, and explain things as you go along. You interpret experiences and events in such a way that others can say "yes I see what you are saying, and I have experienced that too and it is common human experience and common sense". There are no references beyond what are strictly needed to confirm a point, and the dominant and crucial reference point is the person's own human experience and basic logic. In a word, the person's common sense.

Propositions are put to the person and ideas are outlined in simple words, and these are offered to the person to think about. He/she then accepts or rejects or thinks about the ideas. No big deal, no axe to grind, nothing to hide. "That's what I think or am saying; now you make up your own mind". This is the process used in this book. It is an open discussion about some aspects of life, making comments and suggestions and coming up with ideas, to facilitate the reader thinking and making their own assessment of what life is all about.

I don't have the last or second last word on these important issues, but I do have ideas and I share these with the reader. People of all sorts and persuasions have pondered over the meaning of life and of man, and of where science and literature and rationality and belief fit into the picture. Everyone at some stage in their lives wants to know what the truth is. Truth searching is the most basic of human endeavours.

The book is somewhat eclectic in the way it flits from one area or idea to another, and this is done for the purposes of painting a picture rather than engaging in a painstaking methodical process. It is meant to appeal to the heart and mind of the reader, as opposed to a purely cognitive methodical study of reason or the mind. It tries to capture the spontaneity of life in its variety and humour and change. It paints a picture of man in brush strokes that fit into the big picture of what man and woman are. Quotes from philosophy and literature and even popular music are used to highlight points and to underpin ideas and opinions. The book should make an impression, much like an impressionist painting that comes to light from a distance. Something at a deeper level should happen. The reader will like or identify with the underlying theme – that we are created, that we are made to love and believe, that we are eternal, that all we see and experience in life is passing away, and other similar themes. The reader may (on the contrary) be upset and react strongly against the overall impact of the book, but at least he should be able to say that it is a simple transparent and honest attempt to draw back the veil on the meaning of life for everyone.

It may read more like Gary Larson in spots (light hearted and a little zany in its humour), and other times more like a self-opinionated rant (hopefully not!), and here and there like a romantic flight of fancy. Hopefully it doesn't feel like a speech from "the higher moral ground" or preachy lecture. The medicine is real and based on up to date psychology and internal medicine. The philosophy is mainly common sense and metaphysics – the philosophy of being. The psychology is mainstream common sense. The humour is unique!

Contrary views to those expressed in this book are widely publicised and available in books and publications elsewhere, and there is no need to give them more air play in these pages. The views expressed here are not the usually found in "best sellers" in the world of psychology/medicine/philosophy, because scientific and psychological and philosophical books expressing a credible and rational and simple belief in God are not politically correct. They don't get published or read, because they don't generate money and because people have "moved on". People in the Western civilised world do not want to be challenged in this way. They want to be affirmed in their life choices and don't want to be made feel uncomfortable. The many highly publicised books and journals written by unbelieving scientists and atheists and agnostics, get much more marketing than those of believers in these fields. Hence the reason and need to promote what could be called a Christian or theistic view of life, based on the sciences and literature and philosophy and psychology. There is little time spent on opposing views in the book, for the simple reason that they are already over-represented in books and the media.

Some may say "How do you know what you are saying or suggesting is true? What is your proof?" and this is a relevant point. I may not be a world renowned scientist (but stellar scientists may know less about life and philosophy and truth than hard working men or women), but I am putting out a stall in a simple transparent way, and the readers can assess what is said in their own way. What is presented is a coherent view of life based on the normal functioning of the human mind since time began. The existence of God and what that means is also key. It is a prism through which the drama of life certainly makes rational and human sense. The proof of what is presented here is mainly to be found in the lives of millions that have gone before us. It is also found in the transparent common sense that is used. Life is a challenge and it is reflected in these pages. Sometimes it is witty. Sometimes it is understated. Always it has a serious undercurrent trying to get the reader to think for him/herself and see if what is said doesn't make obvious sense. The reader him/herself is the final arbitrar between opposing views.

The ideas expressed in these pages are not like the car sticker on the Maserati in the council housing estate a few years after the economic boom had burst which said "It seemed like a good idea at the time!" They are enduring ideas based on the ideas of the great philosophers of the West – Plato, Aristotle, Aquinas and their schools. They are also a reaction to the facile empty and depressing lore of the modern day atheistic proponents – Dawkins, Hawking, materialists, evolutionists, determinists to mention a few. These writers confuse people and have "nothing" literally to offer them. They have no hope no meaning no joy and no love. The ideas here are mostly based on the witnessed lives of ordinary people who struggle with illness and poverty and loneliness, and who try to understand why. It tries to capture what has rescued them and given them meaning, what helps them to persevere and hope in the future.

WORK

A good place to begin any consideration of what man is, is to ponder about the activity of man. What does man do? The answer is he works. What then is work and what is rest? Is rest a recovery period that enables one to work more and better? Why work? What is the purpose and reason behind the spectrum of work? What causes work and why? What does mankind say about it and what does mankind do about it? *Work* I suppose. Is it body language, the animal equivalent of foraging? Is it a neutral activity like scratching the back of your head, or is it far more meaningful? Is it always painful and tiring and difficult, or can it be rewarding and elevating? Is it optional and can you live happily without it? Work my friends, is here to stay! It is the perennial yoke across the shoulders of mankind. It is the gold standard of a life. A life without work, (unless one is incapacitated in which case work is the effort to get well) is unintelligible. A life full of productive work of service on the other hand is obviously of great worth to the person and to society. All agree?

A big issue is what do you *do* with your life? Why have you got a life? What are you supposed to do? Sit around and play computer games? Watch TV? Stay in bed? What? Are they YES's I am hearing? Then the NO's continue to read but the Yes's better listen in and be ready for a major wake-up call! The reality is that one of the key components of a credible human life is that it is full of work. A car that sits in the garage, a yacht always moored in a harbour, a house unlived in…all these describe obsolescence and futility. Cars are meant to be driven, yachts to be sailed and houses to be lived in. Now ask yourself what is man meant to do? The answer is "he is meant to work". Nowhere in any text or prophesy or wisdom book is it said that "man was put on earth to twiddle the old thumbs and get fat and croak from a heart attack, because low and behold his cholesterol got too high!" Nowhere will you find that! There is an expression that says "only the good die young" but really it should be "only the fat die young" c/o all modern medical research.

If you want to live a productive healthy and longish life you have to work. All medical research shows that suitable work is good for people. They are healthier physically and mentally. Something "right" must therefore be happening when all man's boxes are ticked by work and he is healthier. Proper use of a machine keeps it oiled up and ticking over. A car needs a regular service and a few long spins to keep it right. A house needs to be lived in and regularly heated and repaired if it is to stay in good shape. A garden needs to be sowed and weeded to continue being a garden. An athlete needs to train regularly if he wants to be fit. Fit for purpose is the goal. A combine harvester harvests corn and barley and wheat. It cannot clean carpets or lay tarmac. A thing needs to be used for what it is built for, otherwise it will break. Similarly the human being must be used for what it is meant for, or else it will break. If you did an entry poll at the gate of a cemetery when all the fresh corpses were heading for their plots, and asked them "now tell me about your life" that would be a good way to get "the best way to live" template. Let's go to such a cemetery!

"Hi There! You going down?"

"Surely am. Done all I could and I'm plain flitted away and dead as a door nail. What can I do for ya?"

"Just doing a survey about life and what you all have to say now that you have it done."

"Work for example what do you say 'bout it?"

"Why, hard work never killed no one. (Often heard this yea?). I worked hard all my life and am now 88 years old. I reared 6 kids and 25 grandkids and the wife is still living. Never drank too much and quit smoking when I was 35. You have to work. Sure you would go nuts sitting around the house. You got to control it though. Do what suits you, and what you are good at, and make time to be with the family and to have a break. But work was my life. All my friends were the same. It kept us honest and well, physically and mentally. I've seen guys who lived for work and they lost their wives and families. They thought all to life was their work and gatherin' money and their great name. I've seen others lagging about and not respected by no one and living off the state. Their kids were no better and they always had the poor mouth and not a good word to say 'bout anything. Work was a blessing. It became a great interest and I loved it. Great satisfaction doing

3

a good job and helping out folk as well as you could. It made me feel better and gave me respect for myself and others appreciated me and would ask me to do jobs, and I was glad to do it. Nice talking to you. Good rest now and lay down me weary bones!"

OK nice interview. Here's another hearse.

"HI there can I have a word if you're not in too much of a hurry."

"What?"

"You don't mind me asking a few questions?"

"OK"

"I'm from the University and want to find out what you thought about life and where you think you're going next or doing next (!)."

"Yea. I didn't do much really. Suppose it was ok. Never really worked. Got a drink problem later on. Wife got on my case. Kids a bit of a mess. Glad I'm out of it to be honest."

"If you had to do it all over again would you change anything?"

"Don't know"

"I see."

"Any advice for the folks back home?"

"Whatever." (What is *that* supposed to mean?)

"Thank you. And where next?"

"Don't know, a rest I suppose"

(Yikes little does he know!)

The human body and mind become obsolete and sick if they are not used as they are supposed to be used (as it seems in the case of our last interviewee). People who do nothing become physically and mentally decrepit. They put on weight. They get bored. They drink too much eat too much and get into bad habits. Too much TV and they become brain dead. Too much nothing to do and they get depressed. Too little challenge in life and they become amotivated and lethargic. Eventually they will ask themselves what are they doing and why they are alive. They may have a catastrophic reaction when they meet school friends who have "made a success of their lives" and they ask:

"And what do you *do*?"

"WHAT? What do I doo? Well nothing. What's wrong with that?

(Well, really want to know? There's loads wrong with that. You are a leech on the state for starters. You live on our taxes. You contribute nothing to the common good or the common purse. You get sick and we pay for your free medical care. You neglect your kids and they are all seeing counsellors at our expense. Want more? You give bad example to others who struggle to do an honest day's work and support their family and community.......You are a pest on society")

Is work a punishment? It could seem like that at times but in essence work is activity. It is a goal directed activity which usually has a service element, and nearly always involves effort and toil and struggle. It demands energy and application. You have to focus-in on what you are doing and you have to keep at it. Most jobs are 8 hours a day, 5 days a week. Some are more and some less. Some are assembly line type work, some are pure service, like waitresses and nurses and mechanics. Others are educational like teaching or university work, and others are also providing services like computer companies and farmers. Some is mainly physical like labouring and some is mainly intellectual like research. All work demands effort, and all real work advances the human family in some way. For us work is usually against the grain and could be seen as a punishment of sorts. It would be great if we could do it without the problems and difficulties. We actually like work. That is, we like work we choose, that suits us, and that we are good at. Not all work is like that. Some work is degrading because the terms and conditions are sub-human. Slavery or forced labour or poorly paid work, that has to be done in sub-human conditions, are pure drudgery. They are seriously burdensome and could be called sentences or punishments. Some work is not suited to certain people because it is too onerous or anti-social in its hours, or beyond their capabilities. Despite all the limitations and misfits the majority of people work so it must have a transcendental meaning and it must be very human.

For most people work is a necessity. It is a daily task, unattractive, tiring and necessary. Housewives of the world, farmers, industrial workers assembly line operatives. Blue, white, grey collar workers. Sweat shirt workers. Academics manual workers and artists. All have a common thread. Doing stuff. Service. Making a dollar. But what is it? It is a participation in the dynamic of "act".

The very fact of being alive means we are in action. Our heart beats 72 times a minute (mostly), our lungs expand and contract 14 times a minute, and every little piece of our bodies is "at it" non-stop. We are in perpetual motion. Our brains and minds are being perfused and nourished and renewed, by the blood stream and immune system and other systems we hardly know about. We are ticking over like a well tuned engine. *Work* happens when this engine is harnessed to perform a directed task with a valuable purpose. It is a goal directed activity. It is meant to achieve something useful.

Useful can have varied meanings. It could be service to others, the community, the company or other worthy enterprise. It advances humanity in some way. All genuine work has this characteristic that it improves or supports or advances well being of humanity. A builder builds the city, a teacher teaches the children, and a nurse cares for the sick and so on. If this service element is absent, it is not work in the true sense of the word. Aimless activity with no real purpose or goal could not be called work. If nobody worked the place would fall to rack and ruin. Work keeps the buses moving and the internet on and the dinners on the table.

The planet and all we know changes all the time. Everything changes. All change in the long term is toward chaos. A new baby or plant or car go through a process of maturation and development which seems to contradict the universal law of entropy, (everything tends toward chaos), but age and decay they all do. Fleeting new things sprout up all the time. Work arrests the slide toward chaos (at least temporarily) of our earthly habitat. Life engenders new things constantly, and like a conveyor belt heading toward a precipice, they all inexorably trundle along and get old and fall of the end of the belt and die. They are all recycled and massaged into earth or matter of some basic description, and who knows but they may participate in another life adventure of some form or other…be it a baby or a shrimp or a plastic bottle. This is the great cycle of nature. Someone somewhere is turning the wheel of life and as long as he/ she doesn't get tired the process goes on and on.

You could say that work re-established some order on proceedings. It causes order to happen and it also builds on the chaos. It constructs sustenance and a suitable environment for man and animals and plants. It also expresses hidden functions and applications of basic matter that otherwise would not be manifest. If it were not for man and his work there would be no cars, no cd players no sports stadia. We discover hidden potentialities inherent but untapped in matter like semi-conductors, titanium, and the latest medical scaffold - graphene, to mention a few. We also fill the world with education and books and music and ideas. These are all highly ordered and even beautiful productions. We don't invent as such, we discover what is already there (that is in the world of science). We put order on the treasures of creation. We expose them and exploit them in the good sense of the word. The world of inspiration and the arts is discussed in a later chapter.

Work also has a personal impact on the worker. Some say man was made to work and that he is healthiest and happiest when working. This is true. But what does work do to man? It forges mature personality, it crafts behaviour. It forges discipline. It keeps him out of mischief…it makes a man/woman out of the person, in the sense of giving them stature and responsibility and even power. It is also true that even forced labour or aimless activity may be fruitful and of worth because it is a human being that is doing it. The true value of any activity is the fact that a person does it. The dignity of a human person underpins everything that happens in this world (speaking materially or from an animal level). Work impacts on the doer and on other people and on the planet. A person forced to work long hours or for no pay is a picture of a suffering soul. That person is being punished and as such it moves from the realm of work as we understand it, to that of human suffering. The person involved is very much the key player. What is happening affects him deeply. The objective value of what he is doing may be worthless or of very little worth. The huge effect is on the worker and on his psyche and body and soul or spirit. What would it feel like to be forced to labour in sub-zero temperatures day in day out with little or no food? Millions did this in concentration camps and prisons (and still do). What does that mean? Aleksandr Solzhenitsyn describes this in his books "The Gulag Archipelago" and "A Day in The Life of Ivan Denisovich." Millions endured forced labour over years and still do. This is work but it is also something else. It is severe punishment and degrading of people for whatever reasons.

How do you explain the meaning of solitary confinement? What does such a confined person do? The short answer is he/she suffers. One goes through the psychological and physical degradation these conditions necessarily cause. They assault the spirit and weaken the body. Harrowing accounts of survivors of such camps and confinements testify to the various results of such treatment. The psychological sequelae from detention in Pelican Bay State Prison for example ranged from the panorama of depression, anxiety, panic, psychosis to three to four fold increase in self harming behaviours. Other special souls who survived concentration camps intact were described by Viktor Frankl in his book "Man's Search for Meaning." They had an ulterior goal and reason to want to get out of the camps alive and well. They had a great meaning to their lives and they wanted to get out and continue with them. The nature of human activity in these awful circumstances is not our usual day job. It is serious suffering. It is akin to that experienced by millions who suffer worldwide from poverty, want, illness and the absence of the basic necessities of life. Most of humanity is suffering in this sense. The slums of great cities with their homeless and destitute, the orphaned and hungry in third world countries, and the refugees from war torn countries are just some of these unfortunate people. The rest of humanity who are well and free, mostly work. Those who are not free to work or well enough to work, or who cannot work for other reasons such as those mentioned above, spend their lives surviving and fighting other battles. They are fully engaged in fighting the battles of hunger and thirst, and poverty and heat and cold, and torture to mention a few. These people would willingly work if they were free to do so. As it is they are nailed to their illness or poverty or imprisonment and have to earn their salvation through the means of their suffering.

The lives of those who cannot work due to circumstances beyond their control must have transcendental meaning and value, because they are human beings. Everyone understands that every human life is meaningful and that we are all equal. The CEO of a large multinational is the same as an orphan street child in Mumbai. Both are human person's but with different jobs. The destitute do not build the physical world, they do not contribute ostensibly to the community, they do not build a career or an empire or a company, but their lives have meaning. The vast majority of humanity have as their jobs to suffer. Suffering therefore must be meaningful, it must be activity, and it must achieve some purpose or goal. Much of work is also suffering. It involves effort and fatigue and disappointment and failure and daily grind. It is more understandable however because it produces something. It produces money, and produce and service and a role for the worker and his family, and it advances society and the community. Work and suffering seem to be like hand in glove. Both go together. Some people have more of one than the other and vice versa. So there is plan A (work) and plan B (suffering) and usually a bit of both…and is there a plan C?

Plan C is when you win the Lotto and you do nothing! Well, you go on cruises and holidays. You buy a bigger house and car and keep occupied with interests and leisure.

(Not all people do that – some become philanthropists, or invest or support good projects etc). Plan C is when you sit around and live off your money or the state and basically laze about. Your life lacks purpose and direction and the word "service" is absent from your vocabulary. You spend your life wasting time. What is that? What does that mean? A sheep dog that sits in the barn all day, a machine that doesn't work, and a field that doesn't grow anything are images of useless things. A person that could work and should work and doesn't must be a fault. It is not what we expect. It is not what we respect. It is not a positive for society or the family or the self. Work is a good from the point of view of physical and mental wellbeing, and financial and social wellbeing. To not work when one could means defaulting from these benefits and running the risk of becoming unwell and depending on others for support.

Work could be said to have four effects. The effect on the worker, the effect of production, the effect on others and the effect on the planet. These are all interconnected and good work benefits them all. Is the activity of a thief work? Is planning and carrying out a murder work? Is gossiping work? These outrageous examples are not work. They are activity carried out by humans but they are not work. They detract from society and damage the perpetrators by crossing the moral line toward evil or negative and they do not contribute in a positive way to society. Are worker bees working? Are huskies workers? Are mules workers? They all do things and produce and serve. The bees do it freely but the huskies and mules don't. It is animal activity and since it is not done by a person it cannot be called work as such. It may fulfil the criteria of productivity, and who knows if it has health or other benefits for the animal or bee, but that doesn't make it work. Why not? That is why we need to define what work is. Work as most people understand it is a human thing. It is usually difficult and challenging, demanding effort and perseverance. It has a goal which is usually for the good of society. It is the innate and natural occupation or activity of man. It is man's calling and it is one of the things man was designed for. Sitting on a beach all year, lolling around all the time, being casual or hap hazard about work are sub-human and seem to contradict the essence of man. Work whether mental or physical utilise the brain and body and focus the mind. Work constantly challenges man and gives him rewards and prestige and a sense of self worth. It positions him in society and makes him socially known and located. It gives him rights and responsibilities. It becomes his life - 30, 40, 50 years of hard work must mean something. The same length of time doing nothing must also mean something. Why doesn't everyone just not work? What makes the world go round? - Work.

To continue the tread about the life cycle a moment, we witness the natural process of decline and decay and disorder that is universal and affects everything we know. It is in stark contrast to the astounding intricacy and detail and beauty and advanced nature of even a single cell, not to mention the galaxy or the human brain. How on earth did this awesome complexity which functions like clockwork, ever get into the equation of inexorable decline and decay and progress to disorder and death (which is the main show of life)? How could an aging and rusting world give rise to a beautiful highly complex baby?

This is a major show stopper. How, when everything is getting worse do you get a new anything - and what's more, a highly developed and advanced and living being or plant or rock pool? How does an acorn grow into an oak? This can't be nature in the observed fall and decline of everything model we see all the time. Despite the slow decline in everything we know over time, there seems to be a time capsule somewhere with a warehouse of new stuff that keeps brand new exhilarating beings and things, coming out and walking planet earth for a few years, and then like the earth, getting old and dying. Someone somewhere must be working very hard! Is it that when everything was first made it was all squeaky clean and new and it is all getting old and worn out over time? If we replayed the last n years would everything get new again? Did it have a beginning date? If time is eternity how come it took 'til now to get to this stage? What was before time? Is time just a material thing? Is time a human thing? What is time? Was "the big bang" the beginning of everything, and was everything spanking new at first and is everything progressively getting older and older? Looks like they are.

There are two processes going on all the time. On the one hand at the macro level everything is slowly dying. On the other hand the micro level, new things are being hatched and growing into maturity. Life sprouts from the earth, from the seabed, from living beings. Yet this exuberant power of new life has a "best by date" and it all withers away in time.

We know that nothing happens unless we make it happen. Everything has a cause. That is our human experience. We have to work to make things happen. When we don't work things break and disintegrate and even die. We also see things happening that *we* didn't do. Things like the earth spinning, like the seasons coming and going, like trees and forests and animals appearing and propagating. If mankind hibernated for a few years and reawakened, the planet would still be here. The animals and plants would have continued to grow and spread and die. Who does this? Who keeps the earthly and universal show on the road? …or are we the only ones that roll up our sleeves and work?

That's a problem! We go on our holidays and the place doesn't fall apart. We are capable of some work and development and advancement when all of mankind is at it all day, day in day out. Something else is going on it seems! Someone else is really working super hard 'round the clock! Someone is "working against the clock" to keep the supplies of new stuff coming out, and getting the theatre props of life up and running …before the clock runs out and the world as we know it disappears! The overarching process we witness is the aging and decay of the world and everything that appears at any stage on it. The clock is ticking.

Are there reservoirs of tin and babies and plants in some warehouse deep in the cosmos? The planets and universe is an old man now, and yet it produces shiny metal and succulent lamb and tender leaves. Is there a finite reservoir of new stuff housed in the universe? Are we living on reserves which are finite and will be exhausted some day? The oil wells and water reservoirs are drying up. The total volume or mass or extent of the universe is fixed. This is so because the creation stage is over and we are now in time. We cannot stop the process. We cannot create out of nothing and we are using up all the good stuff, and soon (millions of years?) we will have no new stuff left. The only way this roller coaster of new life and dying life can continue for ever, is if someone creates out of nothing, because the material is all getting very old and worn out. Science and scripture agree. The Big Bang and creation has occurred, and everything that exists has a "best by date" and is slowly disintegrating. The source of life has not failed yet but what keeps it producing? What feeds it? Who designed it? Who drives it? What stops a sinkhole swallowing the whole universe up?

How do you get life out of death? How do you get new out of old? How do you get exquisite delicate detailed design and manufacture and function out of increasing chaos? How do you get extraordinary order out of extraordinary disorder? You throw a wastepaper basket full of rubbish on the floor and come back in 10, 20, 30 years, and….it is still there but even worse. It is now covered with dust, and debris is all around. Just visit a deserted house to see the progressive decay and disorder of what once was a new house. How many millennia do you wait to get a new car or washing machine evolving suddenly or not so suddenly, and popping out of a municipal dump? Who was the last guy to find a brand new Rolex watch evolving spontaneously in a swamp? These "evolutions" are crazy and have never happened and never can happen because nature goes in the opposite direction – toward chaos and decay. You do not get new or designed man made things from rubbish or from earth or from life as we know it. It has never happened. How about a pearl in a shell? Nice one. Well that is amazing but a pearl is sediment (nice sediment) that eventually also decays and deteriorates.

What is old? What is change? Why do things get old why do things change? Why don't things get younger and more fantastic all the time? Is new life just like a death rattle or fragile leaf growing on the trunk of a dying tree? Is the elephant breathing his last and are we just microbes under his nail? Is the show over and are we the terminal strains of a tragedy? In any wilderness or even garden you get disorder if you don't put order on it. You need to plant in lines with patterns to get any order in the garden or wilderness.

In a kindergarten you will reap wild kids and absolute chaos unless you train and enforce discipline. "Someone" must establish order. Order is not natural from our observation and experience. You cannot get the beauty of order and harmony and functionality we see in nature for example, without someone designing and making it *through work*. A head of cabbage does not happen spontaneously! Someone made it. Someone designed it. Someone is a much harder and more powerful worker than we are.

How about the cosmos and the sea and the orbits? Absolutely! "Who" put order on them? That is the question. We didn't because we are too small. A much bigger person must have done it! This macro sized order (of the universe) is also tending toward disorder, as it is all expanding and being blown apart (according to Big Bang theory). Someone must have established order on everything to start with, and ever since that, it is all falling apart. "HE" had better come back and reset the order!

Our experience is that everything dies, everything tends to disorder, and everything gets old. Our experience is that new life emerges all the time. This new life is squeaky new beautiful and highly complicated and designed. This design is not "spontaneous." Nothing is spontaneous in life. How does new exhilaratingly complex life occur…. without a superhuman intelligence doing it? It can't.

You cannot get life from death. (But, it is happening all the time!). You cannot get order from disorder (but ordered things are cropping up all over the place!). You cannot get young from old (but the world is full of young ones!).Where do all the new, ordered, young things come from? The theatre props and the conveyor belt of life are toward aging and death and demise. Where is the source of brand new complicated life and beauty? Is there a white matter zone we don't see? Is there a reality of which we are unaware? Are we seeing the full picture? This emergence of new life from old bottles and rubbish is inexplicable. It should not be happening according to our evidence and experience of the patterns of life here. No one can explain how you get new life. Nothing happens in this life unless someone does it. It seems to us that humans are the only ones putting order on things. No one else is doing it. Even if there is "white matter" it still doesn't answer the question of how it got there and who did it. The spontaneous sprouting of a universe out of nothing is certainly beyond us. Sorry! We are supposed to be talking about work and we are getting side tracked - sort of. We will return to work in a bit.

The animals have their own instinct and patterns (nest building, migration, and hunting) and yes that is against the disorder grain in nature. It could be said that the order humans and animals contribute is only a temporary blip, and once their short time frame is elapsed, the wheels of disorder and entropy take over again and chaos continues.

All permanent and long lasting change in the universe is toward degradation, disorder and decay. There is nothing that does not change. Everything we know and see or experience gets old and decays with time. The present chaos in the climate and global temperature are stark examples of how change occurs. Everything changes because for one thing, everything is temporary. There is nothing that will last forever in this universe. To last forever means either it does not change, or that it is perpetually renewing itself with an everlasting principle driving or powering it. The latter does not seem a credible option and we have no evidence for it. The solar system is in constant change with black spots on the sun, and meteorites, and falling stars, and increasing planetary distances from the sun. We change and die as do all living things. The inanimate things corrode and wear out and disappear. All change means temporality and decay. The world as we know it is passing away!

Anyway this is all apropos of *work*. We suggest that the main activity of man is work. The entire development and advancement of mankind is due to hard work. If no one worked we would die, because we would starve to death. Even the hunter gatherer generations had to work to feed themselves and build living places. Thanks to work we are now in a civilised society with very high living standards. Work therefore improves the living conditions of man. It is a great good. Work is good. Work has enlarged the human mind with all the advances in all the sciences and literature and music etc. It has brought new medicines and cures and has lengthened the average lifespan to eight decades in many countries. It has objectively good effects which can be seen all around.

Work seriously affects the proponents i.e. people. Work fills the time of a person's life (to a large degree). On average a person sleeps a third of their lives, and works a third, and does everything else in the remaining third. You could say therefore that sleep is very important! What is sleep and why so much of it? Maybe we should sleep more! Let's talk about sleep! Only joking.

So getting back to the cemetery to see if we get any light on our discussions so far. I see a hearse pulling in.

"Hi There! Going under?"

"Oh hello. Yes, been there done that!"

"Mind if I ask you a few questions?"

"Sure, fire away."

"What did you work at? And have you any advice to give us about work?"

"Me I never really worked as such. I was orphaned and spent my childhood in homes. Then I was sufferin' with the nerves. Terrible guilt and anxiety and eventually got depressed. I was on a stack of tablets and an injection every two weeks. I couldn't get a place of my own and went from one homeless hostel to another. It was a dog's life. I managed to ward off the drug dealers and stayed clear of drink. So you might say I did my best. How-as-ever I was very sick with the nerves and was in and out of hospitals. The doctors and nurses were great and did their very best for me."

"Good for you. And what do you think about work?"

"I would have loved to have been able to work and have a family and place of my own. It wasn't to be. Never knew my folks. Had one half-brother but we never met much. I was good at making friends and they made life a bit easier. I think I drew the short straw in not being able to work and I envied those who had their health and their house and job and family. I don't bemoan my life, people were very good to me, but it sure wasn't easy. I'm off now to see me maker and maybe He has a little job for me!"

"Great talking to you. Thank you and good rest."

OK we're in luck today here comes a big funeral.

"Good day. Mind if I take a little of your time, I know you're in a hurry!"

"Be delighted. What's another hour when your life is behind you!"

"Thank you. I'm from the university and we are doing a project about work. What did you spend your life doing?"

"I worked as an accountant for 55 years. Had my own business and built it up to be the best in town. I left it to my son."

"Great. And what do you have to say about work?"

"I loved my work. I looked forward to getting into the office and seeing the clients. One day was never the same as he next. I specialised in tax. Don't get me wrong, I had to graft really hard, and work long hours. We often just broke even but we somehow managed to pull through. I couldn't imagine living and not working. How would you survive? How would you fill your time? How would you pay the bills? You couldn't get married or have a family without work. You would end up being penniless and bored if you could stick it. I've seen guys losing it because they had no work. They got depressed and stayed in bed and began to gamble and drink. It was awful to see."

"Yes I see. Do you think man was made to work? Or do you think people who suffer or are in prison or unemployed have a different calling in life?"

"That's a great question. I know that for me work was the backbone of my life. Everything else depended on it to some extent. To suffer from an illness or poverty or homelessness is a big ask. It would be a much harder life I'd say. You would have to struggle every day with pain or sickness or with loneliness, and cold and damp and no place to call your own. To be unemployed is a curse. People don't do well when they have no job. They need an occupation and something to get up for in the morning. It wastes their spirit and they lose self-respect and self-esteem and lose confidence. It is awful to see. I think work improves you as a person. It makes you think and make decisions and plan and take responsibility. You step up to the plate and carry your weight in the job and in society. People know who you are and what you do and you fit in to the town or estate or community. When people know you are an honest and a good worker they respect you and look up to you. You then give good example to the kids and are a sort of role model. This has a very positive knock on effect on the local community. It must be a big challenge to live your life coping with sickness or poverty or unemployment. They are real tests and to survive them and die at peace must be a great achievement."

"That was very helpful. Thank you very much, and have a well earned rest. By the way what happens next?"

"No problem. Hopefully more of the same without the pain."

OK another hearse has just pulled in.

"Hi dear you going down?"

"Why yes honey I'm all done."

"Mind if we talk a bit?"

"Sure. Fire ahead."

"I would like to know how you spent your life and what you now think."

"I worked as a hairdresser, got married, had five kids, and then got back into hairdressing until arthritis took over and I couldn't work anymore."

"Great. Do you think work is important?"

"Well it was a big part of my life. I couldn't have gotten on without it. The friends I made and the money, and it gave me something to do. Rearing the kids was similar. It was work 24/7 and then when they were reared I didn't think twice about going back to hairdressing. I don't know what I would have done without it. It was my life along with my family and husband of course. I guess you have to do something. You just can't sit around doing nothing. I met many people on the job. Some were business women and they really worked a lot. They loved doing what they did. I met teachers and nurses, and apart from stress here and there which we all get they were happy at their work. I met quite a few unemployed girls and those that wanted work were really trying hard to get work, and they would have done anything to escape the boredom of doing nothing. Those that didn't want to work really had sad lives. They got social money and mainly lived in poverty and were not full of the joys of life. I think work or occupation is a must for everyone. How else are you supposed to survive?"

"Thank you."

So all those heading for the cemetery think work is the way to go. They think the suffering option is the short straw and they think having no work is a curse. Sounds very like what we were saying. It seems then that man mirrors nature and the planet, in that things are there for a purpose and function best when used for what they were made. The car is for driving and not for housing chickens, the school for educating kids and not for wintering cows, and a screw driver is for screws and not for taking wax from your ears! The question about man and woman is what are we for? Another way to approach the question is to ask what makes them perform best as human beings? Looking at humanity it become very obvious that those who work in jobs that suit them are the ones who do best.

They are the happiest, most fulfilled, healthiest and live the longest with the healthiest families. Research repeatedly shows this. Work suits man. How much work should you do and what intensity of work and for how many years, are all different for the various jobs and people out there. The quick reply is that you should work at something until you are no longer capable. This could mean and often does that you scale down or change or modify your work as you advance through life. It does not mean that you do nothing. "But here is more to life than work" you may hear. This is of course correct. "What else?" You ask and they say. "You can travel and get a hobby and chill out. Do something different." That is a good point. Do something different. Maybe you can't keep doing your regular job for ever because it is too stressful or you have to retire because of health or contracts. You then look for a job or occupation that suits your age and circumstances. What you don't do is watch TV. All retirement courses say this. Watching TV is a recipe for a poor/terrible retirement. Rest is important. But not 25 years rest! You get bored after three months and want a reason to get up out of bed. You have to do something with your life and that excludes sitting around doing nothing especially in retirement.

The meaning you take from work or suffering or human activity of whatever type is important. If you think work or activity is just to fill the time, and is like a treadmill going nowhere, you could easily be excused for thinking "I'm not doing this anymore. I'll live off the state." Some get away with this but it is not an acceptable option because it would stop everything if everyone did that. Who would support whom? Also it is a cop out and a denial of the intrinsic value of work or of human suffering and of the innate value of human life. If everyone abdicated their roles and responsibilities imagine the knock-on effect on chronically sick. "I'm fed up of this suffering. I'm out of here" could be a reasonable response. "Look at all those healthy folk sitting around doing nothing and having a great time, and here I am with my sickness." Disaster would follow. Therefore not to work or not to suffer are not options. Plan C is a non-starter. We did not invent work or suffering …or humans either. We are born to work or suffer or both, and also to enjoy life. Among the best thrills in life is achieving a goal or doing a really good job or getting recognition for work well done. Also praise and support and empathy for a suffering person is a very welcome thing. The suffering is easier when a person is surrounded by caring staff and family. Friendships and relationships are forged and suffering managed in this way also has a big effect on the carers and friends and family and as such it touches many lives. It has deep meaning.

Ultimately we ask the big question "Why are we here? And what is the purpose of life?" The very fact that work is a good for us, physically and mentally and spiritually, and that suffering is also a good, is a powerful indicator toward a possible meaning. A life of suffering is difficult to understand if there is no long term or superior meaning for it. There has to be a meaning. It does not make sense to think of the unjust nature of lives, when many have everything and an easy life and many more have suffering as their life. Similarly with work. Why should some people work all their lives and others not? It demands an explanation. Either the workers and sufferers are crazy, or else those that do nothing are missing something. We know that the great people in life are the workers and those that suffer. They contribute and advance society and make the world a better place. We never laud the lazy or the idle. They do not contribute. They do not help society. They drag down others. Here we are talking about those who freely decide not to contribute in an ongoing way to society either through their work or their suffering.

Work when embraced and done with as much perfection as possible rewards the worker and society. Human activity that is unjust or immoral cannot be called work because it contravenes the primary laws of nature. It is contrary to the common good and takes away from the goods of others and of society. Crime is a typical example. It is not a legitimate human activity and even though it may be done by a person, it degrades the person instead of improving them. Human activity must be geared toward the common good or the good of the person if it is to be called work.

THE PERFECT PSYCHOLOGY

"We're all nuts! Welcome aboard! We're on the good ship Earth and we don't know where we came from and we don't know where we're a headin'. Be happy. Chill. Life is short! Those that don't agree or have a problem with management here can avail of the life rafts on starboard. The rest please come this way. You are in for the ride of your little lives!"

"Anyone with special needs just take it easy we all have needs! Anyone with ideas different to mine just delete them. Here we are all happy. Hear that? Yes we are really happy. I am in control. I make all decisions, so you all don't have to worry one little bit." (Ok it could be Napoleon, or Stalin, or any dictator). "Simple? Absolutely! Piece of cake! Anyone who thinks they are special come this way, and Tommy will listen to you (and you will either comply or you will be offloaded!). You all got the rule book on entry and now I want for all of ye to sit down and learn it off. Here, is as good as it gets so make the most of it…"

This could be a nightmare, or a delusion of grandeur on the part of the leader, or stark raving reality for the millions who have endured or died in regimes run by autocratic dictators. Life as we know it is awfully imperfect.

Is there anything perfect anywhere? Is a diamond a perfect carbon crystal? Is a nine month old foetus born as a perfect baby? Is a JCB 253 a perfect building site machine? What is perfect? What is the reason for all the imperfections in life? Is quality control an issue and where is the head office?

Perfect, perfect, perfect, can we even imagine what this is? We say an artificial flower is so perfect that it seems real. We calculate the coordinates of a perfect circle as x squared plus y squared equals r squared, c/o Mr Pythagoras. We glow at a perfect sunset. Yes we do intuit what perfect is. It is something flawless. It has no blemishes. It is the prototype for all similar things. It is the model.

Being honest, we realise that most of what happens in life is imperfect. Life is full of mistakes, and errors and accidents. Things do not work as they should. The sun comes up every morning….so far. The tide goes in and out at definite predictable times….so far. The weather report is usually as expected for this country for this time of year….so far. But "the times they are a changin'"…as Bob Dylan sang. The perfect planet, the perfect climate, the perfect universe don't exist, "things they are a changin'"…. Is Armageddon on the way? Is the end of the world for real? Is climate change a fleeting mirage in an everlasting climate of sun and spring times? Is time a ticking clock with a beginning and an end? Is imperfection just a pointer to perfection or a sign of the total destruction of everything, or both? I think its both!

Perfect things are rare. It seems that they do exist. The TV advertisement says that they will get you the perfect smile (if you let them fix your teeth at a good price). The film is called "The Perfect Crime", the weather develops into the perfect storm, and the world darts champion gets the perfect score. Usually we meet nothing perfect from one end of the week to the next. You don't need *perfect* to live and to live well. Why isn't everything perfect? Why is there so much sloppy stuff? The car is manufactured on Friday and it is defective….because often on Fridays the assembly team are distracted and tired, and just want to go home, and so they make mistakes and cause the "Friday car" or "Friday whatever". Hence the success of the food chain called "Thank God It's Friday" because everyone wants to quit work and relax. The rugby team would be perfect if they had a second out-half. The music would be great if the acoustics in the room were better. The garden would be A1 if it had more winter sun. And so on.

Things ain't perfect. What is perfect? Is perfect to us really objective perfection or is it beauty in the eye of the beholder type of thing? Is *perfect* subjective or is there an objective perfection? A new bride thinks her man is the perfect groom ….but no one else thinks it! What is perfect for an individual is a subjective assessment. For the individual that is good enough. It is perfect for them. We all have different tastes in music and art and literature and meals, and we can't all be right, or can we? Yes we can. Perfect is not a vox pop or the rule of the majority. Or as a quiz for Toyota Hiace vans went "Why are Toyota Hiace vans the best vans in the world?" The answer by one unnamed respondent which was not published said:

"because 10,000 gypsies can't be wrong!" (Gypsies in certain countries are known for their ownership of Toyota Hiace vans). There is strength in numbers. But the fact that something is perfect for someone means that that person has achieved a goal in a particular area. That person has experienced perfect for them. They now have a taste for perfect and desire it more in more areas in their lives, and ultimately they want for perfect in their very lives.

Objective perfect could mean a thing has absolute perfection in every detail and aspect. It is perfect through and through. If the whole world thought something was perfect, would it be? The answer could be "they can't all be wrong", but that amounts to the totality of humanity calling it as they see it. They could be wrong. They could be wrong because we don't cause perfect and we don't do perfect. Perfect is just a reflection. It is a shadow or vague imprint of perfection personified. To recap, you can and do get perfect balls and pens and circles and many other things. Going up the food chain to more advanced realities like babies and women and men and deserts and seas…. the proposition gets harder.

It then depends on what you call perfect. It depends on the standards you set. But that is still subjective. The perfect kilogram is a cylindrical hunk of platinum and platinum –iridium alloy. It is housed in a laboratory under stable conditions in Paris, but it is getting heavier all the time! Mercury and carbon dust are settling on it and adding to its weight. The perfect measure of length is the metre and its prototype is also in Paris under strict atmospheric conditions, but it too changes. The new more accurate measurement is gauged by the speed of light. This too will change because everything in the universe is in constant change. These are attempts at objective perfection of sorts. It is like Bobby Fischer playing chess against the MIT Greenblatt computer programme. What is the gold standard for perfection in chess? The problem with this comparison is that Fischer beat the programme on all three occasions he played it. So what is chess-perfect? It seems it is Bobby Fischer. Perfection is something very pleasing to us, we like it. We also like imperfections! We like the dog with three legs because he is cute and we have more affection for him because he is defective. We spoil the Down Syndrome baby because he is needy and lovable and disinhibited. These kids become the pets in the family because everyone loves them because they are so simple and natural. We like mistakes and flaws in people and things provided they are not serious, because it makes them seem more human and quirky and they touch our hearts. We see something of ourselves in these flawed realities. We know we are not perfect. People who think they are perfect are usually obnoxious and also deluded!

Some people say that humility is truth. Muhammad Ali used say "I am the greatest!" The reality is that he was right and spoke the truth, at least when it came to heavyweight boxing. In that sense you would have to say he was telling the truth, but it is also true to say that how you say it, and the acknowledgement of defects he possibly had (being human), are also part of the mix. Usually we know our defects and weak spots and are not deluded about ourselves. We know where we have to improve. We need to be more sociable or affable, or knowledgeable or understanding. Everyone has defects. This may seem strange and the key question is why? Why is there no perfect person? Why are we all defective as human beings? It is often heard that people mellow as they aged or became more simple and approachable and loving. The opposite can also occur. A person can become fixed and obstinate and selfish. These are signs of change for the better or worse. A person may have spent a lifetime trying to be more punctual or caring and after decades they actually achieve some degree of improvement. Life may also harden people into crotchety old sour pusses or dictators who always want their own way. Frank Sinatra was a great singer but "I Did it My Way", his number one hit single, smacks of egocentrism taken to the limit. Not think so? There is one thing having no regrets after a long life because you did the right thing, but there is another type of having no regrets because you had it all your own way.

To imagine the perfect person you would have to include that they were loving, caring, understanding, even tempered, hard-working, humble, generous, never offended, patient, and great to be with and a positive influence on all they met or had anything to do with them. This is a potted version of what a perfect person would look like. I'm sure there are many other attributes you could suggest. To achieve such a status, first of all you would have to examine yourself and see what needed improvement. Establish a baseline and plan how you would develop all the virtues and habits you would need. Work and life and relationships highlight areas in need of improvement in our personalities. They take the rough edges from our egos and personalities and opinions and make us self-knowledgeable and more human and humble. We become more user-friendly. That is of course if we cooperate with the process. We could react and reject correction or personality misunderstandings and not learn from them and not change. That is our call. Many people improve like good wine – with time. As life progresses then with these wheels of motion chipping away at our defects we should become more perfect. We can and do change. We are not carved in stone. We are not perfect kilograms or metres, we can develop a smile, we can stop using expletives, and we can learn to forgive. We are a work in progress. Life must have something to do with our changing for the better. Why are we not perfect from day one? What is all the effort and pain involved in overcoming ourselves and our quirks? It is like the pinch of the sculptor's chisel carving out our perfect shape from the chunk of humanity that we are. Why life is not perfect, why we are not perfect, and why there is pain and suffering, are questions underpinning the meaning of life. Most people think they mean something. Most people attribute spiritual reasons to these facts and the world religions aren't there for nothing. They can't all be wrong!

The perfect psychology is another day's work. Everyone has some character and physical and spiritual defects. Some people seem to have it all - good looks, money and superior intelligence and social graces. They seem to have it all, but close inspection would show imperfections. That is not to debase them but to point out that there is no such thing as a perfect person or psychology. Most of us get by with "good to go" psychology. We are cognitively intact. We have personality characteristics and we get on well enough with others. The perfect psychology really is a reflection of the perfect person. It shines through them and impacts on themselves and others. They are well balanced good to be with, quick to comprehend and understanding and loving and so on. The psychological manuals do not mention the word love. If you type "love" into the search box in the DSM-5 (The American Psychiatric Manual) you will get the following:

No results matching your search were found.
Check your spelling.
Try using synonyms.
Make your search more general…and so on.

If you read the guru on borderline personality disorder Dr John Gunderson (I'm sure he won't object to that title!) he describes the management of this difficulty in personality. He says that by giving the patients a safe place to fall, by encouraging their self-esteem, and inculcating the idea in them that "I am alright; I'm ok and am a loveable guy/gal". This really helps. It is the result of trying to understand another suffering soul, and to empathise with them, and make them feel understood and wanted and supported and listened to. This approach brings healing. It stands to reason because we all feel great when we are understood and picked up and caressed. We *do* love. We understand love and it really goes deep with us and changes us for the better. It actually cures people. To feel alone misunderstood uncared for and rejected is awful. To throw a line to such a person and to empower them to appreciate and respect and care for themselves is a great step forward. It strikes a cord with what makes them tick and what makes us tick. It reaches into their inner world and draws them out and gives them a seat at the table. It enlarges their hearts and makes them feel that they are worthwhile individuals and as good as anybody else. This is truly a great therapy. We do it all the time with our friends and family and with those we love.

Psychology is more than the perfect score on a personality test. It encompasses our way of being and reacting and thinking. To some extent it cannot be captured because it is boundless. Boundless, in the sense of always being capable of more growth or improvement. A perfect IQ, perfect interpersonal skills, perfect motivation and memory, and perfect "emotional intelligence" could all be a "cold" presence. The warmth and attraction and affection of the personality should also shine through the psychology. The kindness in the eye, the calm presence, the witty word, the forgiving smile are expressions of the person and do come through their psychology. It could be said that some may say that psychology is only a dry scientific concept which is graded using established rating scales. Having said that you could add that psychology also includes affect. Affect is the term used to describe the warmth, coolness, suspiciousness, repulsion, fear or other feelings the person arouses or causes in you. Vivacity, dourness, moroseness frivolity and anger are other characteristics and reactions or impacts a person can have that may affect you. The personality and psychology are closely intertwined. Maybe it is best to describe psychology in this sense as "How did the person make you feel? What kind of a person do you think they are? How would you describe them?"

Some people are cold fish, some are all over the place, some are calculating and some are regular guys. The perfect personality/psychology is what we would all like to have. We all know our Achilles heel. We understand we need to improve. We cannot change our brains so we are stuck with our intelligence and personality type. We can tweak our personality and way of being. There is a golf clinic at the Belfry Golf Club in UK home of the Ryder Cup, which boasts that they can get you hitting the ball much farther with your own swing and with a new designed custom built golf club. You don't have to do anything, just show up (and pay the money!) and swing, and they design your new better golf club. A personality clinic on the same terms would be a sell out! We would have our own swing (ourselves and our way of being) and we would get a designer pack that you just drink or eat to make ourselves more perfect! In the real world it may be that a person needs to see Dr John Gunderson, it may be they need a regular counsellor, or it may be that a good self-examination of our behaviour and way of being will be enough to start change. Most people do not need "professional" input to learn how or where to initiate change and improvement. Some do and they do very well by doing so.

After a lifetime of living we know ourselves fairly well. We have tried and struggled to eradicate bad aspects of our personalities and made big efforts to improve other areas. When our personalities are fit for purpose (as most of people's are) it is the daily rough and tumble of life that impacts on us and helps and even forces us to change. Sometimes it is robust. The boss calls us in for an "either or" conversation –either you get your modules in on time or your contract is terminated, type of scenario. This usually forces change. More often we ourselves notice we are grumpy, or late, or superficial or two-faced and we decide to change. Our spouse could ask us to "please stop doing that" and we eventually stop pulling the dog by the tail! Your daughter or son may not be quite as discreet. "Dad will you take off your boots you are bringing mud all over the house." Whatever the correction stimulus, we are being corrected all the time (if we are lucky - they say you only correct someone you love), and we constantly fail in one area or another, and we end up at the gate of the cemetery, still without the perfect personality or psychology. The really big ask in life is other people (provided we don't have other pressing concerns or problems, like gambling, or debt or sickness etc). They constantly impact on us and get into our lives and our heads. In the good sense this is great, because we end up dwelling less on our selves and more on others. They can also seriously challenge us and our own image of ourselves. They make us change and apologise and forgive and love. They can also have the opposite effect and lead us to hate and resent and avoid and harden in our mindsets. How a person takes knocks, and humiliations, and rejection, and even bullying, can be a defining moment in a person's life. The ability to rise above the hit, and to embrace the challenge and take advice and do the right thing, can be enormously beneficial in our personal growth. To react badly to these life challenges can set us back and embitter us, which is not a good for us or anyone. Getting appropriate help can enable us to cope better with life's knocks.

Other people are like us. They are defective. We live with others in close contact, and we work in teams and groups. We need to be able to fit in with the group. That is basic. Being good friends with people and work mates and family is a great achievement. It goes beyond tolerating the others to actually liking and loving them. The perfect personality and psychology eventually morphs into a loveable and loving human being. The really great personalities are like that. They are simple and understanding and supportive and self effacing. You don't have to pick your words and you don't have to worry about what mood they are in today. Their focus of locus is not their ego, but on the contrary, it is other people and how they can serve them and encourage them and make life better for them. This is not our usual screensaver but it could be, with effort and focus and constant improving. Mahatma Gandhi, Mother Teresa, Martin Luther King Jr, Saint John Paul II all were great persons and personalities and psychologies. They were almost as good as it gets with humans. They were larger than life and improved the lives of millions by their own lives of sacrifice and love. These could be the image of the perfect person…and yet they had defects. Could it be that they in turn are faint images of the perfect person, the icon, of real personal perfection? Many religions say God is the Icon or perfect person.

INSPIRATION

Inspiration, creativity, innovation and imagination, seem to hail from the same stable or spectrum. They certainly make the world go round (metaphorically that is). They seem to have a source somewhere and the expression "necessity is the mother of invention" may point us in the right direction to come close to it. Motivation, energy, hard work, try and try again, are also connected to new things. The 10,000 hour rule which says that you can't be an expert at anything unless you spend at least 10,000 hours sweating at it has some truth. A pro golfer, a successful rock band or a gold medallist runner, all have spent at least this amount of time at their craft (so it seems). Undoubtedly they have talent to start with, but like our parents say, it is 90% perspiration and 10% inspiration. Inspiration and genius and creativity seem to grow on the fertile bed of really hard persistent work and application to a task.

Have you ever seen anyone suddenly jumping up and shouting "Eureka" ("I have found it" c/o Mr Archimedes)? Have you ever seen someone have such a moment when their usual occupation was to keep the sofa warm? No!

Their Eureka moment is when they find a last hidden beer in the fridge! Real Eureka's happen to really hard working people. All the scientific/literary/human discoveries, all the Nobel prizes, all the Oscars, all the Gold Medals, were attributed to people who worked constantly, and searched constantly and applied themselves constantly to their occupation. You don't find gold nuggets on the sidewalk (usually). You don't compose symphonies on an electric guitar. You don't produce prize roses in a municipal dump.

Inspiration is also necessary to see the invention or discovery. More broadly said talent is necessary. We have all spent well over the 10,000 hours at our benches working away, but very few of us have discovered anything as such. (Maybe we don't need to). Mozart and Beethoven had a gift. They also had hard work. The world is full of achievers and celebrities. These are not lazy people. They have the common characteristic of being really dedicated people and hard workers. Fortune favours the brave and serendipity and chance favour those who apply themselves to their task.

Inspiration is out of the blue to some extent. We are visited by inspiration. We can't force it. We can accommodate its occurrence and encourage it by sticking to our task one day after another but we are at its mercy. It may or may not arrive. Here we are discussing good innovative ideas that occur to people. Inspiration or genius or creativity as popularly understood. Necessity being the mother of invention also suggests that if you think hard enough you will be inspired. So there may be a graft like aspect to it also. The interesting thing about genius and innovation and discovery is that what is revealed by the worker was actually always there! They were allowed to stumble upon it. Sometimes it comes with the idea. Someone has an idea and they keep following it and excavating it and studying it and they may eventually uncover it or the way to exploit it. How to harvest gas from shale is such a present day endeavour. It is worth billions of dollars and has made landowners into millionaires overnight…because their land was rich in shale. This process of harvesting gas from shale is not new but its massive exploitation is new and demands new techniques and safety measures - hence ingenuity and genius and discovery of new ways of working with it. This is a typical example of hard work and study and an idea working in tandem. Like space travel it begins with an idea and it in turn recruits research and study and trial and error and Eureka, we have lift off. Without the idea it would never happen. Without the idea no one would have the energy or direction to invest time and work into such a project because they wouldn't even have a project. Where do ideas come from you might ask.

To write a symphony a composer like Mozart had to sweat over the score and redraft and fine tune it until it expressed what he wanted to express. His idea of the symphony may have been explicit from the start or it may have developed during the process of writing it. Sometimes writers say they don't know what they are going to write until they actually start to write. Other times they know exactly the plot and just need to express in its best way. Inspiration and ideas seem to be sometimes clear in the workers head and other times they seem to mature and crystallise with graft - with the effort to do something. Granted if a carpenter began to write he may not produce a masterpiece, or if a housewife tried to write a music score she probably wouldn't succeed, which points to the need for the artist or worker to have some affinity with the task and the discipline for starters. The reason why writers do get ideas and plots when they write with an initial tabula-rasa is because they are experts at writing and have a gift. A gift or a talent is a great plus toward success in a field. Most people could probably do most things if they were coached and trained and spent the 10,000 hours. Where there is a will there is a way, sort of thing. If you really want to do something it usually is possible. Sacrifice dedication advice and hard work can move mountains. Most people do not have that kind of time, so even though they could be concert pianists they opt to have a family and day job and tinkle on the ivories in their spare time. There are very few world class anythings who have not dedicated their entire lives to their craft. You could question that degree of dedication and say "is it worth it?" Could you not spend your life being a normal citizen and keep your hand in with the writing or science or music instead of "wasting your whole life just wanting to be the best?" There is more to life than being number one. (Or is there?) This is not to denigrate the spectacular achievements of world number ones in whatever field, and these celebrities somehow manage to do all the other things people have to do as well. They are usually multi-talented – at least some of them. How about world number ones for housekeeping, for doing a regular day's work, for being good company, for generosity, for homemaking? These may be the true forgotten heroes and heroines in our very midst!

Anyway to get back to the ideas and their source. If no one ever had an idea we would still be in the stone-age. We would not have been able to direct our ingenuity toward advancement or success because we would not have the aim or direction to focus on. For example if you had a mad idea you would spend a lifetime at nothing, it would be a wild goose chase yielding fatigue and frustration and no result. However lucky for us the muse or well spring of ideas seems to be fairly reliable. The wheel was discovered in 3-5,000 years BC, the computer in 1960's and the smart phone 5 series in 2015. Everything that was invented or discovered was always there waiting for its unveiling. To say that man actually invented or created a new thing is wrong. We are worker bees and we get lucky because the queen bee shows us something new in the hive. Discovery invention advancement and genius are just the hand of serendipity or providence allowing us to see more of the inner world of nature which was always there. It enables man to apply his reason to realities that were hitherto fore hidden from him. How many more discoveries and inventions lie in store for us to see in the future? We plod along and build on what we know and use new powerful instruments to see more. We did not make these things (space, DNA, neuronal synapses, dark matter....) we were shown them and we recognised them for what they were – great new discoveries. Our intelligence and minds are kitted out in such a way that we follow a scent like a dog and eventually we get the source. We have enquiring minds and we have reason and we want to know more. Hence discovery. If there were no hidden things in nature we would never "discover them". Why is there a veil drawn across nature? Why are there hidden treasures in nature like in a treasure hunt that has man forever following clues and finding new things? Where do the hints about the correct direction to go to find these gems come from? Who inspires composers and writers when they are primed to listen and the see the jewel of a new work of art? *We don't* we are receptors of inspiration and insight and suggestion. We are not the source of new anything. We are not the drivers of creation or invention we are just worker bees or drones!

You may take offense and say this is really a bit much and condescending and how do you know anyway? Quite right. But does it not make obvious sense that the entire process of human history of advancement and discovery is just a withdrawing of the veil from nature? What have we discovered that was not already there waiting to be seen? Yes you have to answer the question about the origin of our intelligence of how it works - piecemeal over the centuries to get to where we are now; and about the treasure trove of nature that we never knew existed. We still have not found out everything. We are mapping the brain. We are mapping the seas and the skies and all the other areas we know nothing about. Why? Why is it all a mystery and shrouded in vagueness and opacity? Why don't we know everything from day one? Why are we not born with a blueprint innately engraved on our psyches of everything that is and why and how it all works? Why not? We are like badgers who forage and burrow at night and who are blind. We are blind or have been. Look at all the stuff we now know that our ancestors never even dreamed of (or maybe they actually did dream it but thought it was a pipe dream)? Dream and your dreams will fall short. It has happened. Men on the moon, space craft to Mars, synthetic ice cream, driverless cars, 24 hour sport on TV! Yes the dream factory and the thought machine directs man and he thinks he is doing it! Man is a pawn with freedom and intelligence but really a small guy. He is being led on a merry dance through nature and time and been given parcels under the Christmas tree like small kids. He unwraps them and thinks he made them and invented them – unlike the child who knows Santa made them and the child is grateful to Santa! Meantime "Santa Claus" is looking down affectionately at man and thinking "Will he ever get it? Will he ever engage the brain that I gave him and come to realise that there is an entire world that he just doesn't see? That there is an entire reality that many simple folk see and understand but that homo-sapiens as he likes to be called just doesn't acknowledge….because he is too full of himself and his own tiny capabilities! What a pain to have to watch these little gods finding things I put there for them and they thinking they grew there out of thin air or that they evolved out of primordial slush. Sure I don't even know what primordial slush is!"

Everything that is attractive and beautiful and an advancement in the history of man over the millennia is a reflection of a major canvas or masterpiece that we see glimpses of as we progress. How big is this canvas? What new delights await us? We are not there yet. Has our well spring for new things dried up? Are we out of ideas? We have not perfected the solar powered car yet. We have not surpassed the great symphonies or works of art. Yet despite the awesome advancement of man we never had so much poverty and pain. So what does it matter that we discover more things in nature, if more and more of humanity is suffering and on the edge of starvation? We have to discover the way to raise all people to the highest level of prosperity and not just the chosen few. Discovery and art and genius are side shows and distractions to the main show and drama, which is the seeking of happiness and fulfilment for the entire human family. That is the nuclear discovery. What have we invented or discovered there? We know how to increase prosperity and we have millennium goals to advance the wellbeing of mankind but we just cannot do it. We keep having wars and fighting and killing. We haven't discovered the panacea to human misery and fratricide. When will the veil be withdrawn from that discovery? You could say that the answer must be there just like it is for science and literature and art. We desperately need to find it before we self destruct!

The real discovery and the real inspiration has to do with man himself. Who is man? What is man? What is his purpose? These are the biggies. The mind of man is the most precious and valuable thing on the planet. It is our holy grail because if we could discover what it is made for we could discover the answer to everything. Hard work and study and research can be great helps in getting inspired but unless "nature" reveals the answer to us we are lost. "Nature" must draw back the curtain for us to see the mind of man in its true reality. It must show us in terms and language we can understand what the mind of man is and what will pacify it and fulfil it. Why is it never at peace? Why does is take so long to discover the wheel, the x-ray, that the world is round? What is the drip feed of data and information about everything all about? What is the end game? In centuries to come will we know everything like Richard Dawkins or Stephen Hawking or Batman?

The mind of man is the discovery and revelation that perhaps millions have already discovered. Many millions of simple downtrodden people maybe discovered or had revealed to them the essence of life; the meaning of life and the reading of the human heart and mind. Only the design team of the human mind can really decipher its purpose and nature. No one on the popular book stands with glossy covers have expressed the true meaning of life. It is perhaps the little people with no big ideas that really sense and appreciate the value of life, and the reason for all the turmoil and suffering of this life…because they were humble and they were ready for it to be revealed to them. They were not distracted by their own brilliance or ideas. They saw the wood for the trees - they focussed on the really important thing in life and were not distracted by other things. You could say that all the Sunflower paintings (Van Gough), all the new inventions, and all the best masterpieces are nothing compared to one man relieving another thirsty man with a cup of cold water. The reason is because this is a truly human gesture and touches a man's heart. This is a language we understand and that can and may affect us deeply if we allow it to. This is not to belittle all the fantastic achievements of mankind to date, and not to belittle the pure brilliance of our composers and artists and writers and scientists, but to starkly state a truth from a higher order. To our eyes a cup of water to a thirsty man may not seem a masterpiece. With a bit of insight we may realise that with more tiny acts of kindness a world of art and invention and detail would gradually appear, which is far more beautiful and meaningful than all the wonders of the natural world. The mind of man can be more touched by a kind smile than a discovery of nature or a philosophical breakthrough. That is if we are sensitive to the affection and humanity shown by one person to another. Our hearts are touched and our spirit is raised and our hope in mankind and life and the future are strengthened, by a caring hand or a kind look. We are human and that is the pinnacle of human communication. We just need to recognise it. Such acts when carried out on a broad scale have the power to transform communities, and this is seen with the impact of charity works in city slums and in the Third World and in countries with high levels of voluntary supports.

The mind of man is very much connected to the heart of man. What really brings true happiness is finding ones meaning in life and fulfilling it. It is listening to ones better instincts and following them and as a result making the right decisions. We don't seem to appreciate that we all die, and what does that mean? We don't plumb the depths of human love and compassion and say what does that mean or point to? Until we ask simple big questions and be prepared to hear the reply we will continue to be blind and deaf to the real discoveries in life. What does it matter to a sick man that someone discovers a wonder of nature? He will suffer and die anyway. What does it matter to a hungry child that Mozart composed 41 symphonies when he will never hear them and will die hungry? What does it matter that broadband is much faster if nobody cares about anybody anymore? The real discovery and only crucial one is that man was made to love and be loved.

These other discoveries are fantastic and important and advance mankind. Everyone can be inspired, and to be ready you do have to put in the 10,000 hours at really trying to find the truth and be open to what it says and demands. Unless a person is open and honest like a child in searching for the true meaning and values in life, and be accepting like a child to hear the answers, then bias and agendas and distraction will cloud the truth. A person will then not see, mainly because they don't want to see. The human mind aspires to truth and fulfilment and it will be frustrated if the truth is not let in. Inspiration and the light of truth shine in on the mind that has not put obstacles in its way. The cup of cold water or the kind deed, or the charity work mean so much because they tell us so much about the mind of man. They hint at love which is the greatest power a person can have.

The fact that love is the greatest power a person has, is a widely accepted affirmation, and has been widely accepted in all cultures and times, and it is unchangeable. This is manifest in the lives of people who have lived happy lives down the ages and who welcome death as a brother and not a grim reaper. Love is the pinnacle of the faculties of the mind and it shows the essence and purpose of the mind of man. It tells us what the mind is ultimately for. It tells us what will fulfil man and what will bring him happiness, and hints at the goal or ultimate target of the mind. In this life, love, human love, is powerful. The ultimate complete satiation of this power forever is something we cannot even imagine. The ecstasy and exhilaration and joy of true love must be the result of the mind working at full tilt. We get a taste for what would really satisfy all our desires and longings. Set this power at its highest level and you see what it does to the lives of those people who really enriched the lives of those who lived or knew them. They spread joy and peace. The nature of love and its degrees are a topic for another chapter. Suffice it to say here that love is the best motivator, the best reward, the best light (which shows things as they truly are) and the best prize for the mind of man. Everything man does is gauged by the yardstick of love. A man's life is worth what his love is worth. Everything a man does is valued by how much love he puts into it. Education, art, discoveries, inventions, compositions, achievements and whatever inspirations there are, are all at the service of love. Love is *the inspiration.*

MUSIC

When you turn up the volume of the radio in the car, it may eventually distract you so much and limit your concentration on driving, that you could crash. There is an optimum sound volume level, beyond which it begins to impair your concentration for doing other things, and at even higher levels it becomes painful and has been used as a form of torture. When music is played in surgical operating theatres the calm and focus of the team is improved. A recent scientific study showed that both the surgeon's performance and the anxiety levels in waking patients were better, when music (that was not too loud or distracting) was played in theatre. Further study showed that a coffee paper cup, or more specifically a Medi-Vac Guardian 12000ml suction canister, acted as a great amplifier when a smart phone (which was playing music), was put into it with the battery near the bottom of the canister! White noise in a library conduces to better concentration and less distractions. Music in a supermarket must be good for shopping because all shopping malls have it.

Music and sound and volume are part and parcel of all our lives, and what must it be like to be tone deaf? To live in a silent world would scare the hell out of most people. We want distraction. We want to multitask. Blaise Pascal the French mathematician and philosopher had a fairly definite take on distraction, expressed in his book Pensees. He basically said that even kings need all kinds of people knocking at their doors and talking to them, to prevent them thinking about themselves and becoming morose. He attributed a large amount of human activity to the purpose of preventing people dwelling on themselves and their predicament in life. Thinking too much about ones life and hardships in life, according to Pascal, is offset and avoided by doing things. We could also attribute some of the same motivation to having noise or music or chatter going on all the time. It distracts us and keeps us from considering our difficult situation in life. It focuses our attention on other things that we enjoy or that entertain us, or that we find relaxing or more palatable than silence.

This is not a major aspect of the reality of music, which as we know is one of the finer things in life. Bird song is also beautiful and the birds like it. The Heavenly court sing a new song that only they can learn (Rev 14). Music is here to stay it seems and the noise of angelic harps is possibly around our next corner (if we crash and die!).

Music is also used as therapy. It is relaxing. Mozart is the only composer of music to be scientifically shown to increase calm. To be sure many others do also but they haven't been studied. Music therefore resonates with the human spirit and touches a cord possibly more of the heart than of the head. Music at funeral removals can move deeply to tears. Music at a wedding can get the heart beating and play on the heart strings. Music in a horror movie can scare you and heighten the drama. The thumping music in the film Jaws has you hiding your eyes even before the shark arrives.

Music can paint a picture like Beethoven's Pastoral Symphony or Vivaldi's Four Seasons. It can arouse hate and anger like heavy metal or tragic opera. It can repeat a message good or bad which gets into your psyche, and depending on your mood and mindset could be great or fatal. "All you need is love" sang the Beatles. Their music in general was positive with excellent melody and lyrics. It would not lead you to do harm or fall into depression. Is the song "Cocaine" by Eric Clapton neutral? Is the song "Suicide is painless" neutral? The point being, that music can engrain itself into your mind with its melody and lyrics, and so it is a powerful means of communication. It often resonates with your mood and thoughts because you put on a particular type of music when it reflects how you feel. It can strengthen moods which can be good if they are good moods and bad if they are bad moods. We all experience this. Sometimes we are in form for a sad song and sometimes something with more joy. It is possible that when you are floating and don't have much conviction about things, a song or album can colour your mindset, and inspire you if it is good or depress you if it is depressing or nihilistic. The same thing happens when reading a book. You can react in various ways. You can stop reading or listening if you find it offensive or boring or immoral. You can keep reading or listening and get wrong ideas and images and urges in your head (if it is a bad book or piece of music). Music can influence us and cast a spell in much the same way as a great painting or a book.

Sometimes (or even always) music reflects society. The present surge in "break up" songs may have something to do with the increasing numbers of relationship break ups. The music connects with the feelings of these people. The great symphonies like those of Tchaikovsky can be written from war situations, and mirror the power and suffering of war. They touch the very core of the person because they grow from the horrors of war when people are at their direst state. Turmoil in the world and in countries can give rise to fantastic creativity in the arts, because the soul of a people is exposed and the literary or musical genius of the composer's express the feelings of their suffering country men and women.

Music is melody and words and rhythm and atmosphere. It is language of many hues and intensities. It can change your mind ("Don't do it without me"); or fire you up to action (Eye of the Tiger – Rocky films); or seduce you into indolence like the music in the elevators in Hawaii! Music is very human. There is a season for everything and also music for everything. Children love to sing. Singers love to sing. Most people love to listen. "I would love to be able to sing like that" is a common expression. One lady was heard to say after a soprano sang "it was arresting!" It would take your breath away. It was so beautiful. We definitely *do* music. It is not vital, you can live without it, but it definitely adds flavour and joy to life.

Why do birds sing? Why don't buffalo sing? Is it a birdy thing? Tom Jones and Eric Clapton and other definitely male singers (who weren't birdy) have the mating call off to a fine art. They are like hippos yawning with the female hippos besotted with their he-man hippo call! They can turn on the base cords and holler the male pitch and it definitely is a masculine thing. Men also do all the other music types as well. They serenade, they pine for lost love, and they beseech her not to go…. Why are the Russian Army band and the German and other Army bands so professional and good? It may have to do with discipline and theme (defence of the nation), and also because they are excellent singers and musicians. Birds are the only animals that sing with such variety and melody and consistency. Does that mean they are more human? Does that mean that all other living things – fish, cattle, cats, dogs…are missing out? Or do they do something that ticks the music box for them? Do they purr to themselves, or grunt rhythmically or blow wind acoustically, and therefore play their own brand of music? Try doing an internet search for this topic and you end up with the pop group The Animals or see images of dogs with head phones on! It really is a neglected or non existent area. The male-female connection is a major theme in the world of music and describes the relationship in all its hues and stages.

I must be stepping on all sorts of musical toes with this "thinking out loud" musing about music, but the purpose of the exercise is to uncover or ponder on the meaning of music and what we can learn about ourselves from it. Meantime I have gotten a rude wake up call by perusing the Stanford Encyclopaedia of Philosophy online, and in particular the entry on the philosophy of music! Worth a look! In a nutshell, there are definitive texts and reference manuals and heated debates about the meaning of music and its many layers. Animal music and popular music are hardly mentioned. It could be said that music, art, and literature reflect and mirror the humanity of people. They are the great communication highways that capture the layers of man and speak to his inner self. Oftentimes it is the atmosphere and context generated by the music that is the key thing – suggesting drama, or humour, or tragedy. Sometimes the words are dominant and the overt and subliminal messages conveyed. Generally it is the total impact of all these elements that give the music its power. The female soprano voice and the high G are probably the pinnacle of what music can do, for many people at least. They are exquisite and piercing in their beauty. People can live for music. They can immerse themselves in music all their lives. It could be a hobby or a job or a way to communicate. Others are "not that musical" and don't have a musical ear.

Music is presumably as old as man himself. The Book of Psalms is a great song book dating back over 2,800 years. It expresses all the panorama of human situation and anguish and remorse and joy and exultation. It is the song of the Jewish people as they worship God and pine for the homeland. It displays the full spectrum of the human spirit and human life and it also elevates it to the sublime and divine. It goes as deep as Hades and as high as Heaven. In between it gathers all the human feelings and hopes and sorrows and sings them out 'til the heart is unburdened and lightened. These songs elevate the spirit and convey real philosophy, and position man in his proper place as a humble sojourner in awe and worship of God, toiling away 'til his time is done. Many were composed by King David and have fed the minds and hearts of Jews and Christians for millennia. They are an example of anthropology in music and act as a catharsis for man the wayfarer.

Other cultures and religions also have their chants and hymns and melodious incantations, and all have the common source and goal of expressing the human spirit and at the same time honouring the Creator, and decanting the chaff and dust from the human soul. The pinnacle of music has to be worship. The kingly courtiers with their lutes and harpsicords and sweet melodies played and composed for the pleasure of the king. The accompanying dance and choreography lent atmosphere and homage to the musical score. Such musicians were the best in the realm and they worked at pleasing the king. A eulogy in honour of the king would also please him but would it have the same impact as a musical piece in his honour? This is debatable. What we can say is that music relaxes and draws you in and changes you and you enjoy it. It goes deep into the mind and massages layers of our psychosoma that engage and captivate us and carry us to a world of other. That is, good music has this effect.

A history of music outlines the role and development of music throughout the ages. It distinguishes cultural differences and instrumental development. The world of sound has always been there. It is becoming more sophisticated perhaps with modern echo chambers and electrical instruments and digital reworking. It still is dependent on a functioning ear for it to be appreciated and this will always be its limitation in some sense. It also depends on the human mind to appreciate it and give it meaning and for it to gain enjoyment. To some extent music and art and literature and fine foods and velvety textures are the same phenomenon. They are playfulness of the senses that capture the mind in their web and carry it away from the hum drum to the exotic and the worlds of inspiration and creativity and carefreeness. They are disarming and force us to leave aside our basic rationality for a while and allow ourselves to be taken on a mystery tour and spoken to. We become more receptive and listen and let our imagination wander. This does us good because it may inspire us and help us to forget our worries and be drawn away from ourselves. Good art and literature and music do this. The faculties of taste and smell and touch do not have the same potency to connect with the mind and subconscious. They haven't the intellectual aspect that hearing and seeing and thinking have. Maybe some animals get carried away by the touch of a craggy rock or by the smell of seaweed or the taste of fresh straw! It is more than being transported to another thought process, it is an intellectual leap and predominantly involves the mind. We appreciate really good art, music and literature because they touch our souls. They communicate in appealing and enjoyable or pleasurable ways with our minds. Our minds are very active while we admire and study a Rembrandt or read a classic or listen to a masterpiece.

These are the top end of the music and art worlds. Meantime in the supermarket heavy metal would drive the customers away so they play easy listening. On the radio it is pop music 24/7. It is catchy (usually) not too deep (!) and has mass appeal. It is distracting melody with basic lyrics that speak to the average housewife or working man. The themes are the themes of their lives. They express in tone and beat the feelings and struggles of the average man or woman. They reflect the day's headlines. They are mainly from the social and personal columns of the daily papers. Is this music? Well it definitely is. It hasn't the sophistication and depth charge capacity of serious classical music, but it may achieve the same or some of the same purpose in its own way. The human spirit needs light relief and fun at times and some types of popular music meet this need admirably.

THE HUMAN MIND REVISITED

The human mind is as good as it gets on planet earth. It is the most sublime and aesthetically beautiful and spiritual reality on earth. It is the soul of the human person. It is a free reality that thinks and loves and dreams largely of its own accord. It is not pre-programmed and "it has a mind of its own", it is free. It goes to sleep and wakes up and does everything with its good friend – the body. The human mind is an enigma. It is like the wind. It comes and goes, we don't know from where it comes and we don't know where it is going. Sometimes it is like a wild colt that has to be bridled and broken-in and trained into a first class race horse, because its passions and drives and thoughts are racing all over the place. Other times it is an abyss of depravity and hate and nihilism. It can be a cauldron of tears and guilt and remorse. It is often a dawn of hope and love and understanding. It is real and accompanies each person on his/her earthly journey.

The human mind exists. It is real. Anyone want to object? If you do not accept the stark raving (and it sometimes is stark raving mad!) reality of our minds then try not thinking for a few minutes! For example, we are aware of it and are conscious of it and recognise that it is *us*. Everyone has a mind! It is ours, and we decide what goes on in it (to an extent). It *is* us. We are our minds. We are also our feet and our gall bladders. The gall bladder may not feel like *me*, and many fair, fertile, fat, flatulent (!), forty year olds (the five "fs" for gall stone problems) become detached from their beloved gall bags when they become diseased, and so I suppose they loose a little of who they are! There is less of them, because they have lost their beloved gall bladders! The heart feels more like me, and I know the eye is me because when I got a sty in it it bothered *me*.

The body and mind, or is it soul (?), are lifelong pals. They should be faithful friends and what is good for one should be good for the other. After all they are like identical twins or Siamese twins. They never ever separate except that is, at death. Let's stick with life. A pain in your foot upsets *you*. You are all foot now because it is getting all your attention and you wish (your mind wishes - not your foot) it would just behave itself and stop being a nuisance. Likewise your mind becomes panicky and agitated, and behold your heart goes out in sympathy with it and begins to beat faster and you begin to sweat (your body). They just do everything together. You may become addicted to alcohol and then both mind and body suffer. It is difficult to isolate the mind as if it were an independent being because it isn't. Mind and body are two sides of the same coin, two aspects of the person. In this life you cannot have a mind without a body. When we speak about the mind we therefore also speak about the body because they are co-dependent in some mysterious way and they are intimately connected. The worlds of psychosomatic medicine and mind-body-spirit attest to this permanent indwelling of mind in body and vice versa.

To stretch the limits a bit "The Bourne Identity" film series starring Matt Damon further complicates the issue. It is exactly the limit, almost, of what it means to be *me*. He doesn't know who he is and is programmed by a computer chip in his body. This could occur! You could become absolutely amnesic and forget who you are and everything about yourself (happens all the time! I have often seen it….!). But, behind all the confusion and haze and doubt you are still "in there", and you are peering out wondering "What is happening? Who am I? I am all over the place. I don't feel right. I forget everything." Your body language and speech and being or behaviour is still very much you ….but the trappings of memory and mental clarity and personal identity are off beam. They are absent. They are missing, but yet *you transcend them. You are you and not your ear or eye or breath or memory or past or future...*You could say "well that's great let's off load all that stuff, I was fed up of it anyway and lets be me!" *Me or you* live in all that material stuff and that psychological suit (our personality) that are designed for us personally. We, you and me, are stuff. We are not free spirits. We are "fat spirits" with feet and heads and teeth and memory and intelligence and drive and passion. You could list all the material a human person has as part of his birthday suit, and you would probably still be missing much of what goes to constitute a regular person. There is hardly a vital organ or mental faculty that we could not do without, and still be ourselves. Where do we really reside? Is it the heart or lung or is it the conscience or frontal lobe? You could replace/excise all of these and we would still exist. It seems that once a human body of whatever state, is alive, be it an amputee in a persistent vegetative state or a newborn encephalitic baby, the person resides in that chunk of respirator supported and heart–lung machine supported body. Matt Damon had no memory or sense of identity and yet it was Matt Damon alright. The lady walking down O Connell St in Dublin, who has just flown in from Atlanta, and who can't say who she is or where she is from, is also present in her skin as *herself.* She is definitely "mixed up" but she acts true to her form and person. It is she alright. Eventually after four weeks hospital and treatment for stress or depression she will be right as rain. Most accident and emergency departments have seen this. It is called hysterical amnesia.

Being "us" may be as much in our left toes as in our zany self-conscious image. We are human - a being of body and soul. The mind understood in this sense is a being or real entity we subjectively experience that is partially under our control and partially not (we can be subject to passions, mental illness, psychoactive substances like drugs or alcohol). It is our inner sanctum or core where we peer out at the world and others and everything from the safe inviolable and hidden shelter of *ourselves.* It is also intrinsically and permanently confluent or immersed and dependent on our bodies, which in their turn depend on the mind to enliven them. No mind equals no body, and in life no body equals no mind.

The brain on the other hand, is the apparatus housing the cognitive faculties and the basic human drives, like hunger and thirst and sex appetite and temperature regulation and our personality. It is another of our body organs. The mind or soul resides in all of our body and it may seem to be mainly in the brain but this has never been proven. The brain seems to be where most of our willing and thinking and dreaming occur. This could be called our mental life and it seems to be closely allied with our destiny and freedom and decisions. You could say that this is the organ that processes such abstract material, but to say it is the mind or the lion's share of the mind has no basis in fact. No one has survived without a brain (so you cannot amputate it like you can with a leg or other organ) and people who are brain dead survive a few days at most. It is an intrinsic and essential part of us but it could be changed for an upgrade! Put the brain out of commission with an anaesthetic, and yet we are still there and put on our brains again when it awakens. We have not gone away. We are always alive and housed in our bodies. Our bodies and brain are part of us but not all of us. We have a vantage point somewhere from which we make the decisions, and experience the ups and downs of what happens to us in the body and brain and mind. We are spiritual with a spirit part and a body part. We need a body, and we are animal in that sense, but we are also spirit. We wear a body and brain and it is us, correct, but not all of us. The sweet spot seems to reside at a distance. It sees all and feels all and thinks all and stays aloof until an executive decision is made, and then we "own up" to it being us and we wear it. We come out, and assume our new position. We live our decision, and it has now become part of who we are.

Let us say we have to decide to marry or not. We say yes, and now our state has changed and now we are married, and Mary/Tom is a huge part of our lives. Our sweet spot acknowledges this change and takes ownership of it and begins to adopt a new me. Our identity has changed and our mind is now launching from a new base. It is no longer only me but my wife Mary is now engrafted or added to my concept or realisation of who *I am.* My self image has changed and now instead of being a single easy going guy/gal, I am a responsible enthralled spouse with a new future and new responsibilities. *Throughout* life our mind changes to accommodate new things that happen to us. These may be personal decisions, like getting married or getting a new job, but often they are happenings of chance. I buy a new car, have a family, get fired, get appendicitis or whatever. All these things impact on *me, my mind, my working understanding and experience of my mind and of me myself.* They now engraft into the new me. They become part of my mind's motherboard and stilt my thinking and the concept I have of myself. I am changing.

"Wow you have changed! Or. My God you haven't changed a bit you are still the same old Tommy I knew 35 years ago." We do change, and even to not change, means we had to struggle not to change. Our minds change throughout life. We change throughout life. Life changes us and our minds. The direction of change depends on many things.

"Do you believe in anything?" This question moves the discussion on toward the core of the human mind. A cat doesn't believe. It knows the dog is bad news. It knows the mouse is where it is at. Animals, bugs and plants just do it. They do not think. They do not rationalise. They can't. Men and women do rationalise and believe. They are presented with information from a source and they either reject it as being untrustworthy, or they trust the person or source and they believe what is said to them, or they partially accept it as possibly being true and reliable, and make a mental note to check it out later. "Do you believe that I love you?" is a question seeking a fulsome response. You could go along with it and say yes and see how it goes, or you could say yes you believe it and let it take you where it wants. This latter full blooded "I believe" is what we are talking about when we discuss belief. The person can and millions do, believe in this sense. They really believe in their spouse, or friend or company or abilities. We have this capacity to engage with a reality and trust in it - hook line and sinker.

You could go through life and not believe in anything that you couldn't prove or find out for yourself. You wouldn't trust anyone or anything without cast iron proof. This mind-set is a lonely place to be. It means that one would isolate oneself and never takes anyone's word for it. One would live life in a super-controlled and narrow minded and bleak way...as life passed by. In a paradoxical way such a view of life shows that they do believe, they believe in themselves and their own views and opinion. They actually do believe, but not in others or God, but in themselves. They also believe (if that is the correct word) in many other things because they use information and science and machines that they don't understand or couldn't obtain themselves, and so are forced to trust others data and work and word if they are to survive. Wouldn't the quality and warmth and vision of their lives be so much richer if they could only believe others (who merited belief) and trust them? Economies depend on mutual trust, on an understanding that good will underpins the business. Labour relations in work disputes is much easier and more successful when there is a degree of mutual trust and respect.

The final frontier for the faculty of belief is when one believes in God. In another chapter we said that the most powerful faculty of the mind was love. What belief does is it focuses this love and also nourishes it. You cannot love what you do not know. The more you know something or someone, the better you can love that thing or person. No one will deny that the mind is capable of "believing". This is amazing and extraordinary. The spectrum of belief is from delusion (where you believe something to be real that in fact is not real); to honest trust in another (believe what someone you trust tells you); to trust in what another tells you even though you find it difficult; to belief in an altogether demanding knowledge that will change your life and make serious demands and sacrifices on you (religious belief). This difficult belief is ultimately dependent on a trust in the person who reveals it to you. You take his/her word for it. Religious belief is even farther down (or up) this line. It is a full adherence and acquiescence to a truth revealed by God, because God says so.

The entire world is based on belief. The society could not function without trust and acceptance of what people tell you. This could be called basic grade belief. Then there are closer relationships like spouses and brothers or sisters, who really know and trust each other. This is a higher grade belief because they know and love each other so well. Then there are the millions and billions of living people who believe in God and who live their lives in accordance with this belief. Counting all the religions there are at present - over 3 billion people believe in God as we speak. That does not count those not religiously affiliated. In other words when you count all those who believe in God it comes to the majority of people now living. This is not a 20ᵗʰ century phenomenon but transcends time and culture. It is a human sign which was and which will always be there.

Such belief brings with it a panorama of new insights and knowledge and understanding. Things fall into place and we grasp the "whys" of our lives and of earthly life. We intuit the causes and reasons for suffering. We see the silver lining of the cloudy life we lead. We sense the end of the rainbow. We live on a higher plane and our love has a new focus. Our faculty of love has a new and altogether sublime and terrible target revealed to us by our belief. It is like a pauper who suddenly becomes aware that a beautiful and powerful woman loves him. He can do many things. He can shy away and say "she's too good and too much for me" and continue to live a pauper's life. He could get to know this lady, and then when pressure is put on him by his peers to reject her and her way of life because of their jealousy or envy or evil, he could succumb and betray her. Or, he could respond to her love. He could allow himself to be led by her and elevated by her and strive to return her love. He would have to wash and shave and speak well and learn courtly behaviour. He would think nothing of this compared to the powerful love of such a beautiful and majestic woman. This woman could elevate him to high honours and position and also he would enjoy her affection and love. This scenario is Cinderella type dreaming. It is only a faint hint however of what the absolute knowledge that belief brings with it and the response of love to this knowledge, can achieve in this life and forever after. Belief in an all powerful and loving Being. Knowledge of an all powerful and loving being. Experience of an all powerful and loving being, when belief and knowledge and response or love all merge into one, is the ultimate goal and prize. It is super natural love.

HOW DO WE WORK?

The human person is a mystery! How do you understand a person? What is a person? I was speaking to a man today and it began to dawn on me as I spoke that we sometimes work top down. We get a hold of ourselves, engage our brain, and cop on! Our friends often say to us "be sensible" and stop getting into a fluster about nothing. This may work and we realise we are over-reacting or giving in to irrational fear or impulses. Our top down pathway stops the spiral of irrational behaviour. The conversation might go something like: "What are you getting upset about? What is the worst thing that can happen? You could become embarrassed in the restaurant, you could shout out in church, you could drop dead. No problem! Just do it...!" Well OK, not that simple. But yes the idea of rationalising about a situation and acting in consequence does make sense. We can do it most of the time and in fact it is how we usually operate. We think something through and then we do it. It is like a football coach preparing for the next game. He watches the videos of the opposition and plans his strategy accordingly. We watch the videos of the opposition in our heads but often we do not act accordingly. Our hearts or our nervous system or our fear or our laziness over-rule our heads or our cognition/ thoughts/reason. We do not do what we think and may even plan to do.

Life is not just pure reason or thought as we all know. Sometimes that just doesn't seem to work. For example we can be so emotional or driven or angry that the thinking part of our brains cannot gain control, and we act out of anger or frustration or impulse. The rational man would love to do X but the human man resists and often gains the upper hand. We then operate according to our passions or instinct or confusion or fear or whatever. We cannot somehow over-ride these powerful drives and we end up acting either for or against our better instincts or thoughts. Tennis players grunt because it gives them more power in their shots. The All Black rugby team perform the Haka as a war dance to get adrenaline flowing and to scare the other team, and to shore up courage and war like aggression. Women hum or sing when they are up to mischief and men growl when they mean business! Our passions really do fire us up to action. "He went mad with rage", "She went dizzy with fright", "He went stupid with hilarity" and so on. Our thought control is out the window when the passions or emotions kick in…or they can be. We can harness our passions or emotions to fortify our thoughts and desires to execute our wishes (like the grunting tennis players or the Haka rugby dance), or else they can take over and get us to do things we never would do in the cool light of day. For this reason the old Irish expression "nature breaks through the eyes of the cat" (Briseann an duchas tri shuile an chait) takes origin. When a person has habits and has repeated acts and thoughts and mindsets, then when the crunch comes and a sudden or decisive response is required, and there is no time to think or work it out, what do you know but a person acts true to form. They do what they always did. They do their usual. They do what has become nature to them and it breaks through their eyes. A cat will always do what a cat does. A person will usually always do what they always did.

That is not to say that people can't or won't change. They can and do change all the time. But it does mark ones card to say that unless one makes a special effort or makes a binding executive decision change will not happen. Such concrete decisions could be: "I will never smoke again from tomorrow at 12 o clock"; "I will never meet that woman again and I will change job and house to ensure it"; I will strive to be at work on time and from tomorrow I will go to bed an hour earlier so as to be up in time." These are credible human decisions that can and do cause change. We can overcome our demons. We can do the impossible or as the notice on the hospital geriatric ward wall said "The impossible is routine, what we depend on are miracles!"

The heart is probably the most powerful source of drive and passion. Give your heart to someone or thing and it will take over your life. It is good to give your heart to your spouse or calling in life or family. To really love them and want the very best for them and to be prepared to do whatever it takes to achieve that. That is heart. The thoughts second this desire of the heart and fashion the ways to achieve the heart's goal. (Illness and brain damage distort the picture because the brain is malfunctioning and so we are discussing normal mental health only in this discussion). We are not computers. Switch on your tablet and wouldn't you be shocked if it told you "where to go", that it wasn't playing today and was in foul humour. Imagine a computer or car having a hissy fit or changing your route or ideas. Machines don't have passions or emotions. They don't have a mind of their own. We design them and they are programmed to do what we decide. In time computers may have attitude given the growth of cookies and tracking, and they may tell you "No you went on that web-site before try this one now", or the sat-nav in the car will say "Stop, stop right now. I'm fed up of that twisty road. You take the motorway for a change!" This is possible because we can set them up to do this.

Who sets us up to do things? Are we designed and programmed? Well yes! We are delivered in a sweet amniotic sac with our very own designer umbilical cord and unique face and feet. We have special designs on our fingers – finger prints. We are computers with attitude. We think. We also laugh and cry. We walk where we want and we socialise with others. Who designed us? Most people have average intelligence and memory and social skills. Most people have the usual range of emotions that fall within the functional range. Most people can have defects in any of these areas that cause them problems. Some get angry easily – they have a short fuse. Some are lazy and they take it easy. Some are obsessional and have to have everything in a certain order. Others are not simple and tell lies. You could go on and on. Everyone somehow has some defects. A psychological assessment could ask "what is your predominant defect?" and if the answer is "I don't have any!" then the predominant defect is obviously lack of self-knowledge or even worse it could be pride. Isn't that bizarre? Everyone has defects. When we find a fault in a product we send it back and either ask for our money back or get a brand new one for free to replace the damaged goods. We are damaged goods and remain damaged until we die. There is no perfect person. That must mean something. It suggests a fault in the source material that went into the making of us all. Else the design is wrong or got broken. Science cannot tell us why we get sick or why we are defective. It can say this is wrong with you and the cure (if there is one) is whatever. But it cannot tell you why you have sick genes or a weak constitution. No human knowledge can answer the question of why there is an original blemish on the human blood line giving rise to illness, and personality defects and death. Religion is the only source of information on this basic question. Interesting!

Most computers do not have defects and they are man-made. It seems that the design team responsible for making men and women - our design team, was asleep on the job since we all are defective! We malfunction all the time. Usually it isn't the cognitive or thought apparatus that is defective but the other faculties. The desires for example which pull us toward what we want but maybe not what is good for us. We *can* actually want or wish. We are self-conscious and know ourselves to some extent. We feel pain. These are way beyond a computer's capacities. A computer acts rigidly according to key stroke commands. (Taking it simply). We often respond to key stroke commands for routine day to day life. Our mind tells us this is what to do and we do it. We also have more powerful engines that may help out or thoughts and put them in to action, or may have a mind of their own and drive us on to act even though we didn't plan it or even think about it. Our desires can do this. Our passions and our emotions can do likewise. A golf swing is almost connatural after years of playing. Riding a bicycle is connatural after many months cycling. We don't have to think about them any more they come automatically. They say (and it is true) that the practical skills are the last to disappear in old age or dementia because they are so co natural or hard wired. I once saw a 90 year old man drive into a geriatric unit in his own car and when he did a mini mental test (normal score is about 25 to 30 out of 30, dementia is 15 to 20 or less) he scored less than 10 on the test! Crazy is putting it mildly - but he could still drive. You wouldn't want to know who is driving behind you these days! His mind was shot as they say but his driving or learnt skill was still intact much like a golf swing or other skill.

This shows that repeated actions build up habits which become hardwired and almost happen automatically. An addict will have to avoid friends if he wants to quit because as soon as he is with the old crowd he will be using drugs again. We associate one thing with another. We hear the 11 o clock bell and we think coffee. We see the street name and think off licence and beer. We go to that shop where she goes and think of her. We have a cascade of associations and triggers that lead on to the target action. This can be very good as well as bad. Meeting a generous soul makes us more generous. Seeing a poor man helps us to forget our worries. Hearing a baby cry brings us home in our thoughts. All of these peripheral associations can gen up our emotions and thoughts to form a desire that we follow or resist depending on circumstances. This locus of desire or want or capacity we have to want to possess is innate. It is powerful. It is in everyone. It can do untold harm or good. It leads us on and directs our lives. Whatever we want we get, almost. We normally craft our desires to what is reasonably attainable and so do not frustrate ourselves. It would be crazy to pine for things we could never get. That would be non conducive to peaceful living. As a result humans do not overextend themselves for will o the wisp desires. If a person is not careful his desire could lead to crime to obtain his booty. This happens all the time.

To recap. We have our rational thoughts and these do most of the hard graft of day to day living. Like a computer or sat-nav we just obey them. Then we have the heart with all its array of faculties that seems to ignite powerhouses of motivation, and desire, and drive, and endurance, and love, and hate, and all the passions. Anger, fear, remorse, guilt, apprehension, resentment and tiredness or lethargy, and hopelessness and despair and hope and faith….to mention a few. Some organ! These are the major players. These are the game changers. They carry all with them and brook no obstacle. They are the king makers and the consummate lovers and the serial killers in our minds. The thought process is a cold clinical cognitive process. These faculties put serious spin on our thoughts and blind us (love is blind…as is hate) and can marshal our thoughts to think what they want us to think. As you think so shall you act is usually our day to day way of working. But it also happens that as you act so shall you think! This is the big one. This is thought control in action. "The dictator is just. Repeat! The dictator is King. Repeat! The dictator is God. Repeat!" After all King Henry VIII said he was Head of the Church of England and you were killed if you didn't take the oath of allegiance. Our history – the history of mankind, is full of thought control and manipulation of thought to satisfy actions. Psychologically speaking you have to justify yourself and your actions to achieve relative peace in your head and be able to function. If you didn't reconcile your thoughts with your actions you would be forever in a state of doubt and unbearable ambivalence and you could not continue to live like that. Nature established the way out of this dilemma and it is the stronger of the two that holds sway. If your thought content or moral compass is sacrosanct then your actions will be forced to reflect this power direction. If you are unsure about your views or morality or conviction, your actions will sway your thoughts to justify and second your actions. As a consequence you begin to "think differently" to please yourself that you are acting correctly or at least to reduce the guilt (when you have done a bad action). Our thoughts are often the handmaids and servants of our will.

The will is the giant in our heads and is the king of the castle and it calls the shots. The wonderful world of neuroplasticity has transformed the way scientists understand the brain. Until relatively recently, 25 years or so, scientists thought the brain was fixed, that it could not change once a certain maturity of years was attained – let's say 20 for argument sake. A quick scan of the internet on the topic of neuroplasticity shows how far we have come. Stimuli can cause brain changes both physical or anatomical and functional or physiological! This plasticity or ability to respond physically to stimuli is right up the alley of freedom and self determination and free will, and everything but determinism. "As I think, so do I change my brain." And the more I think in the same way the more hard wired the circuits become. In other words what books such as "The Brain That Changes Itself" by Norman Doige and the world of neuroplasticity point to is the ever "evolving" shape of our brains, moulded by our response to stimuli. Now as we all know stimuli can come from the north field or south field or anywhere and impact on us. A bit of news, an insult, a failure a success etc. Stimuli can also be and in fact usually are self-generated. We can actually decide and do things due to our free will, and our brains suffer the consequences of these self-produced stimuli. We refuse to sit down, we refuse to speak to someone, we ask a question. These are random free acts initiated and carried out by ourselves. If we freely continue to spend time with a person we like we can cascade a plastic avalanche called love! These enduring circuits, be it of attitudes or habits or love or hate or attachment, require repeated going over the same decisions, to become hardened. This is illustrated by the following example from the book (mentioned above) which has to do with the acquirement of skills. A scientist "mapped" the brains of blind people who were learning Braille. After several sessions the maps reverted to their original zero baseline. However after 9 months effort the maps now configured to a new enduring pattern consistent with a well learned and repeatable skill, that of reading through Braille. This shows that repeated actions and mental effort eventually does lay traces that last, and that now act almost automatically like cycling a bicycle or swinging a golf club or reading Braille. Will power, determination and desire can force us to repeat ideas and drives and passions, and lay down traces of thought and behaviour that become part of how we are and who we are.

This is exactly what free will and personal responsibility would predict and would require of our brains. It is really no surprise that scientists are uncovering this very reality and discovering even more plasticity (flexibility) where once the brain was thought to be a fixed unchanging organ.

The will is exemplified by the experience we have of "I want this and I am going to do it or get it." This may mean "I want this at any cost" or it could mean "I want this if it is possible without too much trouble." There is a spectrum of "willing". We all experience this. "Come hell or high water I will get my way" equates with a resolved will to follow a path. Lesser "willing" is a variation of this power. The expression "to put your mind into something" describes the process of going from a half hearted willing to a more determined focussed willing. Our will is whispered to by our desire and it may accede to it or reject it depending on circumstances. It carries out the desires if it wants to. However the will has the mind at its disposal to trawl through and evaluate the pros and cons of saying yes or no to a proposition or a desire, and the result is an executive decision by the will to accept or reject the action. We all have these "will I won't I" moments and they are usually not life changing. "Will I go this way or that way, will I go out tonight or watch TV? Will I bring an umbrella or not?" The faculty of judgement and the clarity of our thinking and our dispositions all come into play in making decisions.

These three troubadours (heart, will, rationality/reason) come into their own when we have a hard decision to make. When we have the chance to be generous for example. We walk down the street and 50 yards away we see a beggar whom we know. We are not in a generous mood and we cross the street to avoid him. Or we don't mind giving a little money and we keep straight on (our heart and our generosity decide). Or we don't feel like it and we struggle to overcome our mood or thoughts and carry on and either give something (generosity) or pass by and ignore the beggar (harden our hearts). We could excuse ourselves by saying that we support them already through official charity donations, which is a legitimate reply (rationality input). We could also realise this but even still be extra generous and give a few bob as well (head and heart together). This decision touches our pocket and our heart and our reason. At least for many it does. For some it doesn't because they don't care and never give money to beggars anyway (hard heart and don't need to rationalise). All life is there on the street!

Our lives are full of beggars on the street. "Who will mind the kids tonight? Who will prepare lunch on Fri when I am not here? Why should I have to do that, its someone else's job?" A myriad of such tiny details and pulls on our heart strings and keeps us busy. Acts of mercy (visiting the sick; looking after friends; being patient with people; going the extra mile; being understanding and forgiving etc) are tiring but really rewarding and do tax our energy and spirit of humaneness. Being dependable and giving a good service in our jobs is hard at times. We do it out of a sense of responsibility and justice and service. We could get away with doing less but our spirit holds up a higher goal and standard for us to achieve. Our will adheres to this higher way and strives to accomplish it. Because we *want* to.

Moral decisions involving right and wrong also tax our system. We want to do X but our minds and conscience tells us it is wrong. We want the Mazda X 235 sports car but that would mean no holiday for the family and no extras at home. It could be called a selfish choice to get your own way at the expense of others especially loved ones. Your mind may immediately cast this car idea out as unacceptable. It may dally on it and eventually come out against it. Or it could justify itself and say well I do all the work and I need a sports car to relax and they will use it as well …let's get it. We had a holiday last year anyway!

For some a really difficult decision would be if they find out their teenage daughter is pregnant with a Down syndrome baby due to rape. If this were a normal baby in a wanted pregnancy with supportive parents it would be a welcome gift. The baby is the same, it is a human being perhaps not perfect, but viable and innocent. The correct decision is to embrace life always. Many would decide to abort because it is an unmarried young daughter; because it was a rape pregnancy; and because it has trisomy 21. All the panorama of reason and heart and will and judgement and morality are involved in this scenario. The best response is the "its no decision" response of "great news when is she/he due and we will be with you all the way." It never even enters their heads that anything but nature's way and respect for life is the only way. It is not an eyes wide closed decision understood as the following critical attitude to such a response: "What world are they living in? Don't they know the hassle of a handicapped child and the expense and the responsibility and how it will ruin their daughter's life? What kind of people are they? Do they not love their daughter and after all its after a rape? They are callous and stupid!" So the world would speak. Meantime the most basic of all ground rules would have been shattered even without giving it a thought. The ending an innocent life never even enters the world's head. The world does not equate one life with another as being equal. The secular materialistic outlook on life cannot comprehend the logic of cherishing an unplanned and needy baby, because it undervalues the preciousness of a life. It weighs the life of a child in the balance against subordinate issues and deems it unworthy to live.

The reality of having such a child would change life…. for the better! The daughter would learn a most important lesson in life by realising that every life is equal and deserving of respect and support. She would see the safeguarding of the most basic of all human rights – the right to life. She would learn the lesson of sex - that it is a powerful force and gift that has serious terms and conditions. The parents would also be rewarded for their generosity and support of the daughter by a pervasive feeling of having done the right thing, and being happy with their decision. There is also of course the joys that these children nearly always bring to the families that welcome them.

Yes the will usually sifts the thoughts about a project or decision and studies the emotions and analyses everything and eventually decides what it will do. This usually happens in the depths of the soul where the only observer is the self. Ones very self. Ones self-conscious being is like an all seeing eye that watches everything one does and thinks and hears and senses and feels etc, and takes it all in and "thinks about it" and then decides and then acts. A big question! Are we free in all this mental sifting and thinking? Can we do what we want? Yes and no. We can do what we want in the sense that it is possible for us. However there are other constraints that exist. We have a computer – our thoughts and reason. We have an array of moods and passions and feelings. We have our will and our desires. We have our ground rules. Now you have to harness all the mind and thoughts and passions and emotions and will and desire, and get them all working together and in a row and then it is decision and action time. This is routine workaday mental functioning.

However it may sometimes have a sting in the tail when someone suddenly wags a finger and says "Oh! OOOOH! You can't do that!" "Why not?" "Because I said so!!" This is a profound and riveting and definitive endgame. The dictator says no. The boss says no. The wife or husband say no. OK so you do it anyway …and you get away with it, or you don't and you get punished. You do it out of disobedience and the boss kills you. The boss is stronger and has ultimate power over you. These are his ground rules. The computer has to do what it is programmed to do. It has no choice or free will. We have choice and free will. We are not programmed in that sense. We are constrained by rules and regulations and laws. The laws of the state, the terms and conditions of our situation in life (married, single, employed, parent etc). Philosophically we are free and can do whatever we are capable of doing, but practically our freedom is very limited. We are free to do only what we are capable of doing, can afford to do, what is legal to do, and doesn't breach any commitments we have with others or with God. Our will may at times act like an unbridled horse doing whatever it wants, but penalties and punishments and corrections soon school it into obeisance. In reality we usually don't get our own way. The mental faculty of wisdom, whereby we accept ourselves and our limitations and our true worth as they really are, and obey and take advice and correction from legitimate authorities, is a trump card in our minds. It protects us from doing solo runs and living our lives as we want, and not as we should. It is the indelible stamp of veracity on our decisions and lives and says "yes he/she is on course, copy that, lift off." It ensures that our ego is not the centre of our universe, but on the contrary it is dancing to the rhythm of a higher and loftier tune, coming from the jukebox not called desire but love. The ultimate decision beacon we have, whether we acknowledge it or not, is that every decision we make is a decision of love. In a nutshell, love is a giving of our very selves to others and also to God. It is a world view, an attitude, a disposition and a way of living.

For a break let's step into a high street head shop – the shops that have computer programmes to sort your head out!

"Now tell me what you really want." Says the owner.

"I want to be happy. I want to help others a bit. I want a nice house and wife and a few kids. I want 3 holidays a year and 2 cars. I want good health and to retire at 50." "Just gimme a minute, I want to key all this stuff into the computer. Got that. Any more?"

"Let's see what it says."

"Says you have all that already, and it won't make you happy. Say's you are on the wrong programme. Says that you got the happy animal module and what you need to get is "the really happy human disc" or even better the "suffering servant software". OK?"

"Do you sell many of those?"

"Nope! Folks come in for other stuff. Games. Books. Music. Some ask for the seven habits series. Some ask for "Perfect Mind Control" but very few get what you are talking about."

"Why is that? I thought this was a head shop, somewhere you could get a computer simulator or package to sort yourself out."

"It is but most people don't want to do that. They want to be convinced they are doing alright and just want to be endorsed. They don't ask the big questions like, how do I know if I'm doing okay, or how can I do better, or how do I run a check on myself? We have all the packages. We have mindfulness, mindlessness, cognitive distortion and passion restructuring. We do all the mind body spirit stuff. We have a data base from over 20 thousand happy people and that was a hit when we got it first but it hardly sells now."

"Why is that? I thought that is exactly what people would want."

"No it seems there is too much suffering and generosity in it. People don't buy into that kind of life. They say it can't be true. They want something handy that won't stress them too much."

"So you are saying that someone somehow surveyed 20 thousand happy folk and asked them why they were happy and so on and this is what they said?"

"Sure thing. They all scored highly on deep seated happiness, not just the happy animal type. They knew they were happy and they knew why. We did an online survey. We then interviewed them at length individually. They all suffered a fair share. They were by no means wealthy. Those that were, gave most of it away. They were not ego centric or focussed on themselves, but almost always had their minds focussed on others and their wellbeing. Overall they were very simple and honest and good to work with. They were admirable people. Their lives were not at all easy. You wouldn't pick it if you had a choice. The vast majority had a commitment to a religion and the others adhered to what they considered the truth. They understood their lives as a temporary phase on the way to something much better."

"That is scary. These people were from all walks of life, they all suffered, and they all had their focus on others, and they all believed in God as they understood God and in an afterlife. They all had this deep seated intelligent happiness."

"That's correct. Those that bought that disc and liked it and understood it thanked me. They changed their lives and asked me if I looked at it. Truth is I don't have time!"

"I'll take one of those. How much?"

"Twenty five dollars to you sir and if you give me another ten I'd say its made for you!"

This is possible. You could survey thousands of people and classify their degree of fulfilment and joy and describe why they felt that way and what their lives and explanations were. What we usually do (doctors, psychiatrists, mothers, fathers, spouses…..) is ask these sorts of questions about why people are not happy and why they are sad! The world and science literature and literature and film is overflowing with ways to be unhappy. "Tips to be sad". "Get really suicidal in five steps" type of thing. The advertisements and marketing and movies and books all promote false ways to joy. "Get this car, or get this cheap holiday, or eat this souffle etc." Happiness or joy are great indicators that something is going well with you. It is the basic human desire. It drives all our choices and when we choose badly we actually think we are choosing well. Everything we do has this aim. At all costs we want to be happy. Ultimately this is our target. All our top down thought processes and our will power and all our other mental faculties are working hard at it all the time, keeping our ship on the path to happiness. The manoeuvres and obstacles we described above muddy the waters and make it difficult for us to reach port. We have to navigate through the events of life and see the light house and avoid rocks and shipwreck. Our mental harness is geared to get us home but it all needs to be working in harmony and in the correct direction. Happiness is a very powerful and basic human desire and must tell us something about ourselves. Those who are happy in a deep enduring way must have hit the jackpot. Those that are pervasively sad (in the absence of an illness) must have gone wrong somewhere.

FREE WILL – CAUSALITY

Here we all are, a ball of humanity hurtling through space! Man in his habitat is struggling to make ends meet and see what it is all about. We are on this elliptical orbit around the sun. Some seasons cold and some warm and some too warm. If you go too close to the sun you get burned. This journey could go on for ever unless the sun burns out or explodes or more likely unless we get sucked into it and shrivel up! The entire shoot and gallery is on a path to destruction anyway because there is constant change and change always means decay and destruction in this life. Every single thing existing changes and every single thing is dying or becoming defunct and dilapidated and ceasing to exist as it originally did. There is no infinity of energy to keep the planets circling the sun. Where is such a generator and who keeps it topped up and where does the top ups come from? Don't know? Well energy is being expended daily and second by second and the entire contents of the universe are degrading so we have less stock (matter, energy, order) today than yesterday. The primordial newness of everything is slowly fading as we clearly see in the material universe. The only new material is in the life of living things where new creatures and plants replace the old. This is also a finite chain, and every living being uses energy and matter and so the decaying and aging process continues.

Ultimately there is no source of newness, be it animal plant or mineral because we have never found any such source and it would contradict the concepts of time, change, death and the inexorable progress of the universe to chaos and decay. The only way to explain the constant use of energy and the constant change of everything to basic grade matter is to say that the process "started" somehow, and what we are seeing is its petering out (over millions of years). There is no renewal or creation of the universe ongoing. This doesn't exist. It can't exist because philosophy says so, and not science. Science is the nuts and bolts but philosophy is the overarching logic behind the life of everything. Science deals with matter. Philosophy deals with ideas and rationality. Science by definition cannot answer a question about meaning or reasons why things are the way they are. It describes how things are if it is good science but it cannot answer why things are made and why things exist. Philosophy tries to do that.

After that lecture on the universe!... let's talk to man who is the most intelligent being in the universe and see what he thinks! For example what characterizes man? What is his hall mark? If you ask him he is likely to say he wants to be happy. He says he knows life is tough and it is often what you make of it. He says he is free to do mostly what he wants. He can't do everything because for one reason he hasn't got the money, but what is within his range he may do if he so wishes. He says his brain is wired by reason to always search out the causes of things and their meaning. He says this is how everyone that ever lived thinks. He said that without meaning he is just like a robot. He admits to mistakes and to doing things badly. He admits to personality defects. He also admits to getting it right sometimes and that this really gives him a buzz. His wife says the same! I asked him if he thought it was all pre-planned and that he was just ticking the pre-planned boxes (determinism). He said this would wreck his head and if he thought that was the way things were, he would just cop out and give up. He said that was rubbish because it takes the fun and challenge and merit out of life. He said that would make life an automated toy because no one would have any say and we would be brain dead. We would not strive to achieve or to forgive or to love because it would mean nothing…. because we couldn't help it because that would have been our unfree lot. We would not have any say and we might as well plug out the bit of our brains that motivates us and drives us, and that sets goals and targets….because it will happen anyway according to that theory, whether we try or not, because our destiny is already written. You may as well be a battery hen or a dumb animal because that's all that's needed for a plan like that. It would be wasted on us because we are built for more! We are built for freedom and responsibility and merit and punishment and struggle and love. You wouldn't need all that stuff if it is all pre planned and written in stone. So he says.

"You see" he says "the human mind is a high performance machine. It can actually plan and activate its own future and success or failure. That's the whole game." He says. "You got your starter pack and off you go, make the most of it. Life is all about free will." He says he decides all the time and he knows exactly what he is doing. He can go to the pub or home to his wife. He sometimes gives in and goes for a few scoops and then comes home late. He can stay in bed or get up and go to work. He mostly goes to work…but he decides and he has to make the effort and it costs him. His deciding hurts and he knows what is at stake.

This is what you might call the average man's take on freedom and causality and life. The key question is the "why" question. Why is life the way it is? You could come at things from the end and work backwards to see what would give man his truly desired goal or fulfilment, and in this way try to answer the "why." What you might ask would exhilarate and fulfil and make man supremely happy (since happiness is what everyone wants)? What would explain the meaning of everything and man's constant search for meaning? What would explain free will? What would explain man? You could say that the answer is learned in the depths of our being when we strive to live good lives. It matures in our souls and minds (soul and mind are synonymous) as we plod our weary way as best we can. A life of dedication and commitment and adherence to natural law, and constant striving to be a better person, and to honestly search out and acknowledge God, is a sure path to finding the answer to life's meaning. This is a mouthful! It is based on the lives of millions and on our knowledge of how the human mind and psychology and body work. The answer is not so much something you read in books as something you read in your bones after years of working to the bone (sorry). We live the answer and we recognise it and if we are lucky we never let it go.

Let's take the body for starters, because it is easier. The body does well when it exercises and is the correct weight and is not over worked or stressed. It functions well with the correct levels of cholesterol and lipid and all the other nutrients and chemicals. A disciplined life of work is best for the body because experience shows this as do all reputable scientific studies. What is bad for the body on the other hand is a life of idleness and laziness and sedentariness. Unemployment is one of the worst things that can happen to a person. Work, discipline, correct weight, and exercise all go to make the body function well. You may ask what has that got to do with philosophy of life? Many proponents of even contradictory philosophies agree with what we have just said about the body and work. Some of the hardest workers are agnostics and atheists who are convinced that this life is all we have. It is accepted scientifically and humanly that the human factors listed above are good news for the body. These are universally accepted because number one they are true, and number two they don't hurt anyones view of life. The only ones to disagree with this plan are those who want to lay about or don't want to work, or those whose world view includes pampering and spoiling the body. No such philosophy comes immediately to mind except Epicureanism and laziness perhaps!

Dedication and commitment are words we frequently hear when football teams or any sporting teams are being interviewed. We hear that the team members have to be both committed to the team - ethic and plan and goals, and on top of that they have to be dedicated and ready to put in the time and effort. This is a human characteristic of successful enterprises, be they sporting or work related or even human relationships. A person who floats around and is not tied to anyone or place or thing or job is at a loose end. A person with no roots or allegiances or connections is free floating. This is putting it in its starkest image, and there are many lesser variations of this scenario. On the other hand a person who is committed to family and work and locality, and who puts in time and effort into all these pursuits is a connected and located person. He is a solid citizen who can be counted on. He is not a will 'o the wisp or a fly by night. He says what he means and he means what he says. Or at least he has the track record for being a man of his word and his deeds. These aspects of belonging and community and social cohesion and responsibility and fulfilment and identity are important human virtues. They signify a mature reliable person. The opposite is a frivolous unreliable superficial person who drifts through life. Such a person needs help to anchor his life and to mature.

Adherence to natural law is something we all recognise and do to varying degrees. We normally don't kill or steal or abuse or assault or seriously lie. Some do. We have an innate sense of right and wrong and this is the trace or presence of "natural law" in our hearts and minds. When we adhere to what we sense is true and good we do well. When we contravene basic laws of morality like the 10 commandments we do badly. We know when we are wrong because we feel guilty or ashamed or remorseful. We sense that we have crossed some line. We know we have done wrong. That is of course provided we haven't anaesthetized our conscience and mind with denial or repeated wrong doing without remorse, or because we want to do what we want whatever our inner sense tells us.

That is, we don't care what is right or wrong. Most people do care and have a sense of natural law and morality. The world of ethics and rules and laws and regulation is all based to some extent on the basic foundation of natural law. We have choice or freedom when it comes to adherence to natural law or not. We can decide to "do our own thing" and disregard our innate conscience and the laws of the state and of proper living. We exercise this freedom all of the time and especially in the privacy of our own minds. Why is it good to live by these tenets of natural law? One reason is because experience shows that when people live according to upright principles it is good for them and for others and for society. People feel happier and this spreads. They do not offend others and actually do good to others. This has a knock on effect on the bigger human family with positive ramifications for all. When people do not live according to the natural law they end up frustrated because they are denying their own nature. They offend others because their own wants and desires come first and if others get in the way its tough luck for them. They don't value the common good and they cannot because they deny their own common good or natural good. To strive to be a better person is what the challenge of life is about. It is impossible to stand still. Life does not allow stalling and you either swim against the current or you get carried with it. The basic animal tendency for man is to sink to the lowest level of self-gratification and to give into all his basic urges and desires. Life by its nature forces man out of this lethargy and forces him to work and keep up appearances at the very least. It gets him out of bed! Next come the pulls on his generosity and conscience to be a better man. To serve and help out and to contribute to his family and society.

This is being a better person and this requires effort and trial and is a lifelong task. This drama keeps man focussed on what matters and on the positives. It keeps him away from sloth and time wasting and developing bad habits which could and do ruin him. Look at all the idlers, and thieves and swindlers and those that are professional criminals. Hard working people who are trying to get by and improve their lot are usually upright positive people who contribute to society.

Finally an honest search for the power behind life is a noble and just human attribute. Everyone wants to know why life and man are the way they, are but not everyone is honest and open to the truth. What is truth? You could say that truth is what is real. We understand "real" because if you have a nice car or a nice spouse or a pain in your back you know these things are real, because they really affect you. They also affect all your senses and are endorsed by your innate grasp of reality and existence. These are fundamental things we do not have to prove. They are primary or basic facts which underpin the entire life of man. If you deny these facts – the realness and reliability of our 5 senses and our grasp of reality and innate recognition of reality, you cannot discuss anything. The reason is because these are the building blocks of rationality upon which are based all our intellectual life. A person has a need and obligation to use these faculties to search out the meaning of life and the correct way to live, and to strive to find the power or mind behind it all.

Alternatively you could see what results and what kind of fruits and lives the various philosophies result in, and what they have to offer. What kind of lives do those who live according to free will and causality and reason have? (Good, fulfilled and rewarding lives). What kind of life do those who don't accept free will or causality or honest reason have? (Confused and aimless and troubled lives). What do determinists have to offer for life and what is their level of joy or fulfilment? (Robotic animal existences where the die is cast before you can even get a life). What do relativists have to offer and what drives them? (Anchorless drifting from one self-concocted view of life to another). What do atheists have to offer and is it credible or attractive? (Eat drink and be merry for tomorrow you will die). You look at the various options and see what they *do* to people. So you take what is attractive and what fulfils man best and gives him the optimum life, and then you look at the philosophical or rational basis of it, and buy into it. Eventually after studying the lives of the various livers of the various philosophical world views, will you be surprised to find that it is logic and honest reason and adherence to the natural law and belief in a "higher power", that engenders the most fulfilled and happy people? This is also the most coherent and the best explanation for life. No you would not be surprised! Ultimately an open mind willing to accept reason for what it is and honesty and simplicity to follow where it points or leads is the way to go. A biased closed mind on the other hand will filter out ideas and reasons it doesn't want. This is common human experience. Carpe Diem, and search out the really attractive exponents of life. Follow the happy generous and peaceful folk and you will find you are hanging around with the right crowd.

AS WE WERE SAYING.........

Are the world we live in and the experience of living, the daily news headlines and the weather report real "things"? Are *we* real? What is real?... Get the idea? *We* are at blind man's buff bumping into "things" and "people" and getting all worked up about "ideas" and about "who said what to whom". Maybe its all a mirage. Maybe its all unreal. Maybe we are taking ourselves way too seriously. Maybe nothing matters and even, maybe nothing exists! Maybe there is no real objective truth. Maybe our minds could be wired to another language instead of rationality much like computers have Java or GameMonkey Script or Blue! We could be flotsam and getsam driven by some wind or current with absolutely no say and no control and no destiny! How do we know we exist? What is "exist?" How do we know how we are supposed to function?

Okaay! You could rightly say that this man is having a bad day and needs a stiff expresso or Jack Daniels! But, we have all heard this type of nihilism before. Usually it occurs at university coffee tables or young people's discussion groups, but book shelves in top stores are full of such material. Contemporary music is full of the big questions.

"What is the soul for?" "What is a man?" "Love is true its me and you." Or how about "Step into the serene soul." These are all 2015 song lyrics. We have all donned the 3-D glasses and navel gazed into our inner soul/mind have asked "what's it all about?" We have all tried to evade the "in your face" honesty and simplicity of the 4 year old's questions – "Mammy why was I born? Mammy why do you cry? Daddy who is God? Daddy what is love?" (OK maybe the last question is a bit precocious for a 4 year old but then let's say a 14 year old!). The whirlwind of life as we experience it. The terrible news we hear on a daily basis on the media – 7 million refugees from Syria; 100 shot by Boko Harem; student burnt to bone in Halloween party prank – impacts somewhere and somehow on us. It may be a will o' the wisp news flash or deep thought, but we get over it and "life goes on." This may not occur however. We may stay in the moment and dwell on what is actually happening. We may allow ourselves to be touched or moved by the suffering of others, and the *reality* of what we are hearing and seeing and witnessing. We may just hold that deep thought about the meaning of life and let it develop. We may get <u>real</u> just once and cut through the waffle, and we may just get serious and say "What does that mean? I am truly upset and moved and affected deeply by what I have just seen on TV."

We could take a moment and overview the past and the present and the future. We *know* there are 7 billion humans alive. We know most are suffering. We know billions are hungry have no water and live in poverty. We know the hospitals are full of sick people. We know in Ireland that 500 die in road crashes every year. We know there are 10,000 methadone users here also and so on.

We know everyone that ever lived has died. We know the history of mankind is one of wars and famines and pestilence and violence, and that what has happened since the dawn of history will continue to occur.....because man is the same as he/she always was. All of this must mean something. We definitely are affected by it. We even cry at weepy movies. We identify with soap opera characters. We get attached to dogs and cats and even pet rodents! Whatever else, these are "real" feelings and thoughts, and they surely get us going and do something to us. If a guy comes up and shoots your pet dog tell me that isn't real!

The examples mentioned above are mainly or completely negative and show the "bad" side of man. However they do point up the concepts of *knowing* and *realness*. They force one to acknowledge, that whatever about the philosophy and the world view on life one has, the experience and witnessing of it all can and does cut us to the quick. We could even say that we never get over the experience of life. Life events change us and make us different. We don't need to define real, or prove real, because as far as we are concerned it is all real for us. We are not cardboard cut outs or observers of cctv monitors, we are the actual guys living the roles and suffering the consequences. We are real players and our faculties tell us, and our experience proves to us, that we really know things and that these things are real for us, at any rate. The truth about all of this is that life and things and knowing and experiences seriously affect us as human beings, and as such their ontological or philosophical nature doesn't matter. Everything may be imaginary and ephemeral - even ourselves (!), but that doesn't change the fact that we suffer and we learn and we enjoy, and we experience and we are affected and are changed by all that stuff. We matter. We may not exist and everything we experience and sense and see may not exist - taken from a philosophical point of view - because we cannot prove our own rationality and being. We did not invent ourselves or our reason or mind. We were gifted with all this and like a child who never doubts his existence we also should not doubt our given faculties and we have to accept what *is*.

The good news is that there is also a silver lining to mankind. There are the heroes and great people who saved lives - like the 103 year old man who was honoured in UK last week (at his funeral) for saving the lives of hundreds of Jews during the war. There are the charity workers that house the homeless, feed the hungry and comfort the afflicted. There are the fantastic parents who sacrifice themselves for their families. There are the workers who do an honest day's work. There are the millions who love others. There are the billions who believe.

All the above is like a cascade of human life passing through the prism of the universal person. The totality of everything that ever happened, funnelling through the universal man/woman, is what we are considering. Slates falling off roofs, musical harmonies, turbulent weather, smells, whatever (!) all parading into and out of this universal man causing him to change. He might smile at a funny incident, he might frown at a devious event, he might go quiet and think a universal thought. He might scratch his universal ass! Meantime there outside the door is the universal camel eating whatever camels eat and displaying universal camel behaviour. There is the universal sky and the universal tree doing their things.

It just goes on and on. There is nothing new on the face of the earth. What has been, will be again and so on 'til.........what? OH! Never thought of that! For now let's say 'til the end. There is some discussion about the beginning and the end of life on earth but we will skip over this for the present. Getting back to man, he gets all this "experience" of life over thousands of years (there is no definite consensus or proof for how long man is around) and what does that mean? Does anyone disagree and say this is all imaginary and doesn't exist and "depends on how you look at it?" Answer - put a hand into a bowl of boiling water, and count to ten!

The big issue here is how do we know we exist? How do we know the universal man went through all the past and experienced it like we do? How do we know our "minds" are genuine and "truthful" and correspond to "reality"? The answer of course is that we don't know in a profound absolute sense. We have a hunch that we are real, we have innate senses and instincts that guide us. We intuit from experience and we have our rationality. Our minds, believe it or not, did not exist at one stage. Everyone gets a mind when they are born. We don't know where it comes from or Who made it, but every person has a mind and they all work the same. That is unless they are injured or defective. But all healthy minds work in the same way. Isn't that amazing? We just take them as a given. We had no say in it. We are as we are, and life is at it is and things are as they are, and that's our launching pad. We don't have to prove we know, and we don't have to prove that we or anything exists. Since we weren't at the beginning and generation stage of life, but are part of and the result of it, we must be humble enough to accept this, and embrace and learn from what we were given, and not question its reality. We know we know, and we know we are, and let's move on. The ultimate and cast iron proof and explanation for everything comes when the designer of everything shows his hand.

We can see the hand of the designer in his handiwork in the same way as we recognise an artist from his pictures. We see the family features in the children. We see the composer in his music. Why cannot we see the designer in the universe? We can! The entire cosmos from galaxies to nano-medicine is a masterpiece, and that's a serious understatement. The designer of everything knows everything and unless He gives us a steer we are blind to ant understanding.

A dog definitely cannot write a book. Agreed? A horse cannot sing the blues. A car cannot paint a house. And man, what can and what cannot he do? What is man made for? The stark raving reality (?) is that a young man and woman can go away for a while, and low and behold when they come back they have a mini human being, a baby. You ask them how they did it and they smile and say "it just happened." They did not make it, they are absolutely certain of that. They are as amazed as we are! The fact is that the human person is a gift. The origin (… of the species?? Ring a bell?) of man is a mystery. We are as we are. We cannot say how it all began or Who does it or Who made us or what for. From a purely human point of view that is the truth. Now what we all have are these "ideas" like truth, realness, love, hate, right, wrong, pain, suffering, joy and so on. We did not invent these things. So you have to ask Who did?

Ok. We are where we are. We have all these "things" (ideas experiences etc) and we have a rational mind that can "think" and work out cause and effect. We find that when we work like that from cause to effect, that sort of "reasoning" actually works and gives answers that are true and function in our world. The entire world of science and human advancement is based on this activity we call rationality or reasoning. You could throw up your universal hands and say enough of this I'm going fishing. I'm out of here and am not going to think. Plenty of people do that. They cop out. They refuse to follow rationality to where it leads. They get a sniff of where it might lead and jump ship before it gets a chance to look them in the eye. We can do that, we can disengage and just refuse to think deeply. We can live out our lives without ever considering the big issues. There is another reaction to these types of considerations, and that is to twist them and mix error with truth. Many do this. Books and songs and all types of human philosophy and reasonings are out there, trying to hoodwink the universal man into thinking x is y and "that's not the way it is at all."

The undermining of the human mind is a perennial project and the debunking of rationality is a key part of this. If you can say the human mind is amorphous or ambiguous or not rational you are into a new world. It means you have met the universal man and told him "Hey this thinking business and the vision you have of life is all wrong. Its different. You see, we are all free and everyone can think what they like and they are all true and right. There is no such thing as objective truth or reality." And the universal man who has hard earned his spurs over thousands of years, and knows a fake when he sees one says "I see what you are saying. I hear you. And you know what? You are nuts. I've been around thousands of years. I've seen holocausts and death. I've seen love and joy. Don't tell me how to suck eggs. You're full of waffle and deceit. You are shaping your theories and ideas to bend reality to your wants. That's not the way it is. What is real is real. We are fashioned to grasp that and to analyse that and to understand that. What is bedrock is not the human mind (in one sense) but material reality – apples and winds and mountains and birdsong. They "are" and a broken arm "is" and the human mind gotta accept that and work from that, or else it is a lie. When the mind adheres to what is true and real and beautiful it then mirrors reality and is true, and let's say objective."

Eventually we just have to accept ourselves the way we are and where we are and how we are, and work from there. We work with our minds and in particular with our reason. You cannot prove we exist or for that matter that a cup exists…..because these propositions are tautologies or crazy, because everyone knows and sees already that we exist and that the cup exists. Reason is not supposed to second guess itself. Reason is for sifting what is not known to illumine the unknown for us with its logic. It doesn't know what to do when confronted with a known datum. It is the wrong tool for understanding what we already know. The tools we need to understand man are much "deeper" and more subtle. Ultimately it is the faculty of wisdom that gives man the heads up about everything. The entire panorama of the mind and life and experience of the universal man when "looked at" causes one to say "ah ha" and to "draw ones own conclusions". You are not forced to accept what you see. You are left free.

When the headlights of a car glare into your eyes you look down or shield your eyes. However you would never say they weren't bright or light. When the universal picture of man is coming at you it isn't glaring, it is a soft light you can look at, but you can also look away, you can shield your eyes, but you cannot change the light. What is, is. You can also deny that there is light and you can misinterpret the light and say it is something else. This is the axis around which the mind of the universal man turns. That is why there is such disagreement about life and its meaning and what is right and wrong etc. If we all agreed it would be great. When we all see a blue taxi we agree it is a blue taxi. When we all see an eclipse of the sun we all agree it is an eclipse, and those who disagree are discounted as either blind or crazy. But when we all see the universal man we do not all agree. In fact the volume of divergent opinions about him is staggering. Therefore this means either that the history and the consistency and stability of the universal human experience and mind are not true and real (which is not the case) or else people are seeing what "they want to see."

It is like the joke about the animals in the zoo. The animals got sick and an advertisement went into the local paper looking for people to work in the zoo. Several people came and were asked to put on monkey suits and bear suits etc and act like the animals. This went very well and no one spotted the difference between the real animals and the fakes until......one day the "monkey" was so into his role that he swung right out of his cage into the lion's den. People were aghast. What would happen to the poor monkey? The lion approached the scared monkey and closed in on him. Then to everyones surprise he whispered into the monkey's ear "if you don't cool down we'll all get fired!" The universal man is swinging around his cage (the world) and he is not a fake. The people outside the cage may think he is a monkey dressed up in a man suit...... but that's their problem. They are wrong. He really is a man.

This capacity we have to not see what is real and true and beautiful is called denial. We are free to be simple and honest and transparent, but if we don't want to acknowledge reality we can save face and deny it. To a certain extent nobody will know and we won't be embarrassed in public. This is the essence of freedom. In ordinary daily life we can live in denial but we are often caught out. Someone may see us doing what we said we didn't do, or a camera catches us in action, or a court and witnesses expose and uncover our denial. In our inner world and in our acknowledgement of truth, this may not happen and we could be forever living in denial of what is really true. It all has to do with our dispositions to be honest and simple/humble in confronting truth. It may not suit us that gravity exists, or that day always follows night or that pets die, but we are forced to accept these realities, unless we are deluded. With ideas concerning truthfulness, the origin of man and the world, the terms and conditions attached to man's life (what he can and cannot do), the evidence or forcefulness for acquiescence is more "personal." "Everyone is entitled to their opinions" type of situation. This is the nub and basis of why there is so much disagreement about the nature and origin and destiny of man. You can believe and accept whatever you want to and you won't look a fool. This would all be fine if there were no truth and realness about man, and if the whole issue was one of opinion. There is truth and realness about man and each person has to find this. There is truth and reality about material things like apples and hairs and violins. They are exactly what they are and can only do what they can do. The universal man knows all about truth and reality because he is thousands of lives and centuries old, and has lived it all and received the consequence of "truth living" or "denial living." The universal man like the universal soldier has good and bad in him. Every soldier is personified in the idea of the universal soldier. Every man/woman is not captured in the idea or extant form of the universal man in some senses, because after death there is a bit of a shake down. The triumphant man rises up, scars and all, and takes his place at the podium of truth and reality and glory. The other part of mankind who lived in denial of truth and reality are also represented but don't get to share the podium (because they never accepted it existed), and they have nothing to say. The real universal man is the personification of those people who lived in the truth and reality of life and battled against all the pulls and enticements to deny truth and reality and beauty, and they held firm. Some people call these the saints.